The Diary
of a
Cotswold Parson

The Reverend FRANCIS EDWARD WITTS

The Diary

of a

Cotswold Parson

Chosen, Edited
and
Introduced
by

DAVID VEREY

Alan Sutton
1978

Published by Alan Sutton, Dursley, Gloucestershire.
Distributed in Great Britain by EP Publishing Limited
East Ardsley, Wakefield.

First published 1978
Copyright©in diary extracts Francis Witts 1978
Copyright©in introduction, notes and this selection,
David Verey 1978

ISBN 0 904387 19 4

Printed in Great Britain by Redwood Burn Limited
Trowbridge & Esher.
Bound by Cedric Chivers Limited, Bath.

ACKNOWLEDGEMENTS

My thanks are chiefly due to Mr. Francis Witts for generously allowing me to edit some of the diaries of his great-great-grand-father; and to his mother Mrs. F.V.B. Witts for her kindness in making the volumes available as I required them, and to Mr. Alan Sutton for publishing them.

I am very grateful to Miss Sandra Raphael for making the index and to Mr. Brian Smith and his kind staff at the Records Office, Shire Hall Gloucester and to Professor Patrick McGrath and Mr. Geoffrey Sanders for encouragement. I would also thank Mrs. Gretchen Langford and Mrs. Erica-Mary Sanford for kindly typing my manuscripts.

David Verey

Barnsley House,
Barnsley,
Gloucestershire.

August, 1977

Foreword

I am most grateful to David Verey — and I am sure my great-great-grandfather would be too — for the kind and expert way in which he has introduced and edited these diaries. If they have been too long hidden within the family, now at any rate, I am happy to say, they are presented to the interested reader by a Gloucestershire scholar of great distinction, fully qualified to guide us through the squarson world of F.E. Witts.

When David Verey started on the diaries some two years ago, I was living in Cairo. Now that I am back, he has inspired me to read the diaries myself, and I was amused to find F.E. Witts in January 1845 reading Lane's "Manners, Customs etc. of the Modern Egyptians", though not on Sundays. Lane's modern Egyptian has not changed too much in 130 years, and, in many ways, as David Verey says, nor has Gloucestershire.

F.E. Witts would be pleased, I hope, to find today one great-great-granddaughter (my cousin Nancy Kennard) Chairman of the Bench at Stow-on-the-Wold and another (my sister Diana) a missionary in Kenya. If he felt it strange that his magisterial and Church roles seemed to have been inherited by his female descendants, one could add that, since the last war, three of his great-grandsons have been Gloucestershire County Councillors, all commuters from different parts of the county to Gloucester.

For myself, if I am not Rector of Upper Slaughter, I do share with the Bishop of Gloucester the Advowson for what is now the Benefice of Upper and Lower Slaughter with Eyford and Naunton; I have walked from Upper Slaughter to Cheltenham in January (with others, on a sponsored walk to raise money for Cheltenham Hospital) when the weather was atrocious and my face was "coated with ice" (see 25.1.1823); and I am a banker, of which I hope he would approve, given his own long-standing connection with Stow Provident Bank.

I hope he would approve too that I have turned his rectory into an hotel. It would be a shock no doubt, but he was a practical and sympathetic man (and quite a frequenter of inns himself), and I trust would understand the economic reasons and appreciate that the house was still in his family's hands and well cared for and enjoyed.

I am sure these diaries will give pleasure to many. I certainly hope so. I hope too they may inspire a few readers to keep diaries themselves: that would certainly please F.E. Witts.

Upper Slaughter
Rogation Sunday 1978

Francis E.B. Witts

Illustrations

6

Introduction

To read the topographical parts of a diary, written mostly in the second quarter of the nineteenth century by a Cotswold parson, has for me been a fascinating experience even though Witts is no Kilvert, and perhaps because I know Gloucestershire rather well topographically. It is exciting to see loved and familiar places with different eyes in an earlier world. The extraordinary thing is how little has changed, outwardly; the Three Choirs Festival, Stow Fair, rookshooting the second week in May, are all familiar. My own social experiences of this century are not altogether so unlike Francis Witts's. I have waited on the Judges, as High Sheriff, to take them to the Assizes with my chaplain Canon Keble. My wife and I have dined out, and even the names of the people at the dinner parties have sometimes been the same; we have hunted, we have fished the little rivers, or been out looking for wild flowers. I have never been down Coopers Hill on a snowy day in a coach; but as a boy I have been past Prinknash with cold feet in a bus on my way to Cheltenham to have a riding lesson at Mrs. Parry's indoor school in Regent Street. Other people in Gloucestershire may have this same feeling of affinity with Francis Witts. I hope so. Everyone who lives in Gloucestershire must have been to Cheltenham to go shopping, even if they have not been to Gloucester to go to a service in the Cathedral, though the Dean encourages country parishioners to do so.

It is certainly possible however to live in the county, particularly on the Cotswolds, and not feel any special connections with Gloucester itself. Francis Witts is the perfect advocate for the city and county because his life-long activities took place in both. He was an early commuter, often spending the entire week in Gloucester, and returning from Saturday to Monday to Upper Slaughter to take his duty on Sunday.

Fortunately also, in order to get from Upper Slaughter to Gloucester he had to pass through Cheltenham on his way. Cheltenham was building during the whole thirty-year period of the

Francis Edward Witts as a child

Witts diaries from which I quote. He kept a diary long before 1820 but I have only made extracts from 1820 to 1852. Witts observed Cheltenham's progress. For most of the period his every move required a horse of some kind or another, and it was only during the last part that he was able to go by train from Cheltenham to Gloucester. The fact that travel by coach and carriage was so quick and efficient is to us amazing, particularly when conveying mail, for the posts indeed seem to have been sometimes quicker than they are today, and Witts always received and dispatched letters on Sundays at Upper Slaughter.

Upper Slaughter is still a remote village in the high North Cotswolds, as it was during Francis Witts's life; but even then there were sufficient educated neighbours to form a cultured society, though most of them, albeit, were clergymen. This was the heyday of the upper-class clergy, and many of them were squarsons like Witts, but where he gained over some of his neighbours was in his constant visits to Gloucester where he met all the County figures as well. In addition to this he was wealthy and had financial interests and property in the North of England and in London. Some of this came from his wife Margaret and her well-to-do mother Jane Backhouse. Margaret seems to have been something of an invalid and Francis Witts did most things without her, although he was always affectionate and they had the great mutual interest of their adored only son. He also got on extremely well with his mother-in-law, with whom he lodged while in Gloucester, until she left Wellington Parade and went to live with them at Upper Slaughter.

Francis Witts left some ninety notebooks of perfectly legibly written diary, and maybe he confided his daily activities to his diary rather than to his wife. It must have occupied quite a considerable time in his very busy life, as he wrote at unnecessary length to our way of thinking. To make every point twice may be good practice in a sermon, but not in a diary. In making my extracts therefore I have had to reduce his verbosity — though not I hope his wit — for the sake of our readers. I have also endeavoured to use only those passages which illuminate the history of the city and county of Gloucester, paying special attention to the people Witts met, for they were the breath of life and Witts was a sociable being. Particulars of his day-to-day work, which take up the greater part of what he wrote, have, therefore, to some extent been excluded from these pages, owing to a certain dryness and greater suitability for the serious social historian, as have also the descriptions of his travels in other parts of England which do not have any direct application to Gloucestershire. I have tried to include his descriptions of the countryside and of the country houses he visited round Gloucester, particularly Prinknash, where he was a constant visitor to the Howell family, and Lydney where he often stayed with the Bathursts, and describes the Forest of Dean at length.

Thomas Jones Howell was Witts's most admired and intimate friend. He succeeded to Prinknash in 1815 when his father died aged 47. He was then 22, and undertook the continuation of the *State Trials* begun by his father, reaching vol. 33 in 1826, the year Storer engraved Prinknash. His grandfather, who had interests in Jamaica, and had bought Prinknash in 1770, and entertained there such people as Horace Walpole, Lord Torrington and Samuel Lysons, died in 1802 and was buried in Gloucester Cathedral. His father Thomas Bayly Howell, a lawyer, seems to have been responsible for the handsome classical windows in Abbot Parker's great hall in Prinknash, besides other improvements. Thomas Jones Howell was successively Judge Advocate of the Forces and of the Admiralty Court in Gibraltar, 1822; Secretary of the Commission for colonial enquiry, 1830; Commissioner for the West India Islands Relief 1832; and Inspector of Factories under the Factories Regulation Act 1833, a post he held for 25 years till his death. He married Susan Maria, daughter of Alexander Hume MacLeod of Harris and by her he had seven sons and three daughters. The diary records many moments of happiness and sorrow to this family.

The Rev. Francis Edward Witts, J.P., D.L., was born at Cheltenham on 26 February 1783 and died at Upper Slaughter on 18 August 1854, aged 71. He was the son of Edward Witts of Swerford Park. He married in 1808, and was Rector of Upper Slaughter from 1808 till 1854, and Vicar of Stanway from 1814 till 1854. His only son, Edward Francis Witts was born in 1813, and was his curate at Stanway from 1840 till 1854, and married Sophia Vavasour, daughter of the Rector of Stow-on-the-Wold. Apphia Lady Lyttelton was sister to Witts's father. She was a great influence on the diarist, and had herself a romantic life. Engaged to her cousin, she sailed for India in 1769 to marry him; but on arrival in Bombay, learnt that he had died a year previously. She then married Joseph Peach, the Governor of Calcutta, who died six months later, so she returned to England, a rich widow, and married Thomas, Lord Lyttelton. He died in 1779 at the early age of 35, leaving her £1,000 a year for life. She lived comfortably for the rest of her life in Malvern, where she called her house Peachfield Lodge, after her first husband. The house, which survives, was frequently visited by the diarist and his son.

Witts succeeded his uncle the Rev. Ferdinando Tracy Travell as rector of Upper Slaughter. His grand-mother, Agnes Travell's mother, had been a Tracy of Stanway. The Travells and the Wittses both had houses at Swerford near Chipping Norton. Witts bought the lordship of the Manor of Upper Slaughter in 1852. His son Edward in 1854, and his grandson Broome Witts in 1886, were also rectors of Upper Slaughter, and his great-great-grandson, another Francis Witts, retains the lordship of the manor and other property in the parish today.

The diarist Francis Witts was an active Magistrate, attending Quarter Sessions at Gloucester regularly. He was for many years Chairman of their Committee of Accounts, which then controlled the County finances and rates. He was also a member of many other of their committees, a turnpike trust, and trustee and manager of Stow Provident Bank. He occasionally presided at one of the Court of Quarter Sessions. He was also a most regular attender at Petty Sessions, and Chairman of the Board of Guardians for Stow district from 1836 till his death.

It was common practice at that time for Church of England clergymen to be prominent among the ranks of magistrates. Other magistrates were generally noblemen or landed gentry, with a few exceptions from the commercial or manufacturing class. The magistrate had criminal jurisdiction over offences ranging from the smallest misdemeanour to serious crimes for which transportation was the sentence. The constable would bring to him (sometimes to his own parlour) suspected vagrants, paupers, poachers, thieves, deserters, the mothers of bastard children, people guilty of assaults or threatened murder, drunkards, rioters and anyone else who had fallen foul of the law. If the case fell within his jurisdiction to act alone the magistrate had such remedies as fining, placing in the stocks, whipping, binding over with securities to appear at the Quarter Sessions or Assizes, committal to the House of Correction, or to set free with a vagrant pass. In addition, the magistrate was concerned with local administration, including rating, maintenance of the highways, questions of poor relief and licensing. Attendance at Quarter Sessions also fell to his lot, where he would meet with other magistrates and discuss matters of public administration concerning the whole county, as well as hearing criminal proceedings and appeals.

In the early days the magistrates would meet at the King's Head Inn, Gloucester, at 10 o'clock and then proceed to the Booth Hall. The Sessions usually lasted between three and six days. The general county administration was heard at the King's Head. This included the appointing of jurors and fining those who did not attend, the appointing of constables, appeals against removal orders, matters concerning public works such as highway, rating, the employment and relief of paupers and appeals from Magistrates' courts about bastardy orders. The public court of justice was then held, usually the following day at the Booth Hall and subsequently at the new Shire Hall where the first court was held at Michaelmas 1816. At this court, criminal cases were heard, referred from Petty Sessions, and in some cases the felons were transported; also appeals against conviction in the magistrates' court were heard. These Quarter Sessions provided a valuable opportunity for magistrates from all over the County to meet and discuss their work.*

From the diaries it can be seen how conscientious and hard-working Witts was. The very volume of work covered was considerable and his accounts of it are meticulously kept. We can only admire a man who devoted such a large part of his life to voluntary public service, and the frequently unpleasant experiences which went with it. On June 15 1837, for instance, Witts records the suicide of an unfortunate youth he had put in the lock-up, at the same moment as his own son was happily botanizing in Cirencester Park. It is a telling contrast, which then and for long afterwards was accepted as inevitable, and Witts's comment is not sympathetic to the dead man. In this, perhaps, there is a fundamental difference of outlook between then and now.

Francis Witts's churchmanship would, I suppose, be called "broad". He was always punctilious about taking his Sunday duty. One of the few sermons of his own, which he quotes in his diary, was delivered at the Visitation of Bishop Monk to Chipping Campden on August 18, 1841. In it can be found his whole philosophical attitude to his profession. "The teaching and preaching of the gospel is entrusted by God to frail and fallible mortals, and there are dangers besetting the clergy in their intercourse with the world, both in regards to its pleasures and its business". He speaks of the "undue love of worldly praise, and popularity, as aimed at in various styles of preaching — of amusements and intercourse with society." He disapproved of clergymen hunting; but he was thoroughly sociable and a great diner-out. He considers the extent to which the clergy may take a

---

* See Eileen J. Hart. *Gloucestershire Historical Studies,* VII (1976)

part in politics — his interests were openly Tory, and he mentions the discharge of magisterial duties, and administration of other civil concerns, at both of which he laboured with unflagging energy all his life. He concludes by "enforcing three checks to the frailty of our nature, self-examination, prayer, and professional study". He was a great reader of philosophical books and other men's sermons.

Witts records what the Bishop said at Chipping Campden which included "some temperate, well-balanced, guarded, and not unkindly strictures on the principles emanating from the authors of the *Tracts for the Times,* cautioning his clergy on the subject, expressing fear as to the result of the inculcation of the tenets of that school of divinity; but giving the leading characters in the movement credit for their great learning and high character for piety and morality, and speaking with affection and respect for those members of the clerical body in his own diocese of Gloucester and Bristol, who uphold the opinions in question".

Of these, we know, there were more than a few particularly among the clergy surrounding Tom Keble at Bisley. Sir George Prevost, Bart. was the first of a line of exceptional curates, followed by his brother-in-law Isaac Williams. They greatly influenced the future of the Church of England.

In the following year, 1842, a tractarian Mr. Barker was appointed incumbent at Bledington in the Stow rural-deanery, and the Bishop required Witts and Canon Ford to suggest he give up practises likely to breed controversy. Barker would not, however, discontinue the daily public service he had instituted.

Witts ends his diary for this day in his usual way which is most endearing to anyone who is intimate with the roads of Gloucestershire. "My son (the charming and faithful Edward) accompanied me, walking with me up the hill from Campden, and riding by my carriage till I reached the Worcester road." Here Edward would have had to say good night in order to get home to Stanway. "It was dark when I arrived at Stow, and lighted my lamps."

A typical Sunday at this period is described as follows. "Morning prayers. Visited the Sunday School. Afternoon prayers and a sermon on the attributes of God. Engaged with two parishioners in making out a claim for one of them to a reward to be bestowed for good character, length of service and independence of parochial relief, at the coming anniversary of the newly instituted Stow and Chipping Norton Agricultural Society. Read a sermon to the family (his wife and mother-in-law). An interview with Mr. A.M. by his request on the painful subject of his father's misbehaviour. Oppressed with a heavy cold and cough.''

In 1839 Edward Witts (and his wife Sophy) moved to Stanway as curate. His father's previous curate at Stanway, Frederick Aston, had become vicar of Northleach. Edward, who had just escaped for the first time from his parents' closest scrutiny into another diocese, naturally did not wish to move back after only a few months, and put up quite a good fight. However, the heavy guns of both sets of parents were brought to bear, and the unfortunate couple were forced to submit "cheerfully", particularly as the diarist showed signs of becoming offended.

It was very soon after the diarist had been excessively offended with his fellow magistrates at Stow, the Rev. Canon Richard Ford and the Dean of Gloucester, about a trivial turnpike matter. In his mood of self destruction Francis Witts threatened to resign all his official posts as a magistrate, and it took an abject appeal from the Lord Lieutenant, Lord Segrave, to bring him round, combined with the most tactful administrations of a neighbour, Mr. Pole of Wyck Hill House.

In this close-set community, the rural deanery of Stow, Richard Ford, who was rural dean, had several times had the misfortune to irritate Francis Witts, not least when he spelt Sophy Vavasour's name without the u on her marriage licence, and then went away on holiday, thus causing the near postponement of Edward's wedding. The father was determined the mistake must be corrected, and poor Edward was forced to ride to Gloucester at the eleventh hour to get it put right.

After his mother-in-law Mrs. Backhouse's death on Nov. 14 1842. Witts took his wife for a change of scene to Cheltenham. They stayed in lodgings at No. 3 The Promenade and were attended by their footman, groom, and Margaret's maid Emily Peard. On the first day Witts had a long interview with Mr Gyde one of the Cheltenham magistrates recently appointed by Lord Fitzhardinge, formerly a grocer. "Poor man! He has no peace, and is so thin skinned as hardly to have a sound spot about him."

Witts noticed the changes in the town. A Unitarian Chapel in Byzantine or Romanesque style being built at the foot of old Well Walk; the Proprietary College in Pointed architecture on the Bath Road, "a thriving institution under the influential and popular Mr. Close," with "boys of all ages in academical caps going to or returning from their Classes: and the extensive ranges of houses and detached villas, in all imaginable styles which have sprung up in Lansdown to accommodate the many resident gentry whom the so called 'Queen of Watering places' attracts."

With his son and daughter-in-law he pays a visit to friends in The Park, a new *rus in urbe* which "I have never before visited, and which is still in an unfinished state", and "not distant from the new church dedicated to St. Philip." Another time they drive to Charlton Kings and admire the "handsome villas in this pretty valley,"and he also notices the church here has a "Catherine wheel window" like the one in the parish church. They also visit the shop of George Lewis the monumental sculptor, and order a tablet for Mrs. Backhouse to go in the chancel of Upper Slaughter, a marble framed in a pinnacled pointed niche of Painswick stone. They admire too the enjoyable residences at Prestbury especially Mr. Edwards's Tudor parsonage (this was the height of the Tudor fashion). During Lord Ellenborough's absence as Governor General of India his house at Southam Delabere was occupied by one of his brothers. "It was a glorious evening and a brilliant sun-set for the time of year (Dec. 3rd) ... and the venerable old house was bathed in its full radiance."

St. Mary's church on Sunday was as usual very crowded and they had much difficulty in obtaining seats. "Mr. Close preached extempore with much of his known fluency, self-possession, impressiveness, and ability ... The body of his sermon was argumentative, against the Millenarians. Great numbers of communicants of every class, old and young, male and female, rich and poor, servants and artizans attended, and although the words of administration were not pronounced individually the service was of very long continuance: begun at 11 a.m. it was not concluded till a quarter to 3 p.m." The indefatigable Wittses, however, then attended a service at Christ Church. It was quite dark before they got home for dinner. "There are great spiritual advantages to be had in the town", says one of George Eliot's characters in *Middlemarch.*

Francis Witts showed great aptitude for hard work both physical and mental throughout his life. His prodigious rides will fill us with astonishment and admiration. Upper Slaughter is very hilly and the departure from his stables towards Cheltenham was always up a considerable hill. He was also a practical farmer, and one can imagine how knowledgable he was on all country matters.

My selection of quotations has been to some extent arbitrary and subjective. I have aimed at painting a spectrum of Witts's social life and not his working life, which would require a more serious study of which I am not capable. Being an architectural historian myself I have tried to include references to specific buildings, and such things as monuments in the cathedral and churches. For the first time we discover that the architect of the famous Pittville Pump-room, Forbes, was sentenced to transportation for life for fraud.

The general interest, however, lies more in the people and contacts Witts made. Unlike the famous diarist Kilvert he does not savour each unique experience. Only once does he record that he needed a glass of negus. On the other hand he had far wider contacts than Kilvert, and his references for instance to the widow of Warren Hastings, and to the bibliophile Sir Thomas Phillipps, or to Dr. Warneford, enable us to form more complete pictures of these historical figures. I was not attracted to Witts's problems as a trustee of the otherwise unknown Hunt family, nor to the complaints of Mrs. Dolphin, one of his parishioners, about her husband, both which subjects take up many pages of diary. I hope, however, that I will have helped the historian to cross the t and dot the i in some cases.

At the end of the eighteenth century, historians tell us, the ancient city of Gloucester was as undisturbed by the French revolution as by the coming English industrial revolution. "The ordered perfection of the Cotswolds, the sombre solitude of the Forest of Dean, the distant view of the Welsh mountains provided a fitting backdrop to the essentially rural activities of a market economy." Yet life in Gloucester was not devoid of movement and vitality. Gordon L. Goodman quotes an un-published contemporary memoir, in the *Transactions of the Bristol & Gloucestershire Archaeological Society*, Vol. 84. "There must have been immense traffic along Westgate Street which was pitched with great egg-shaped limestone pebbles, over which rattled some thirty or forty daily stage coaches and carriers' waggons. Processions of mules and donkeys came in from the Forest carrying loads of charcoal and coal, and there were trains of pack-horses bringing country produce from the Welsh border, and in harvest times families of Welsh and Irish reapers."

In 1814 Thomas Rudge in the *History & Antiquities of Gloucester* tells us that the largest single source of employment was the pin-making industry which occupied 1,500 people in or just outside the city. However, the city's economic strength lay in her market position giving access to the industrial wealth of South Wales. Gloucester was situated next the first bridge over the Severn, linking Wales with England. Against this, however, the city suffered from some natural disadvantages. The immediate country round about was too flat for mill industries requiring water-falls;

its situation was too far from the coast of South Wales to compete with Bristol, and as a resort it was rapidly eclipsed by the sudden rise of its much younger sister Cheltenham. Nevertheless, there was a modest increase in population and building during the first three decades of the nineteenth century.

Gloucester's population grew from 7,261 in 1801 to 11,933 in 1831. The most important new area was hopefully called the Spa, and its satellites Brunswick Square and Montpellier Place. No less elegant were the houses built along the London Road, such as Wellington Parade, where Witts's mother-in-law had her house, also in Worcester Street, and the Bristol Road, all catering to the new mercantile and professional wealth of the city.

Most of the economic growth was due to the expanded traffic at the port of Gloucester following the completion of the Gloucester & Berkeley Canal in 1827. In the first year of operation the canal handled 106,966 tons of traffic with receipts of £2,836. By 1831 the tonnage had increased to 323,344 while the receipts had increased to £10,879. Because economic interests coincided, co-operation and uncontested elections should have accompanied this era of stability; but this was not so. Against this background of modest expansion politics were often turbulent. Elections were contested, and therefore expensive to the candidates.

The Corporation of Gloucester was Whig throughout the eighteenth century, and remained so until 1835. In 1789 Gloucester's two M.P.'s were John Webb, a clothier from Painswick, who represented the interests of the Corporation plus those of the eleventh Duke of Norfolk, and an independant called Barrow who died in that year. The Duke of Norfolk's unlikely association with Gloucester was due to his Duchess, who was a Scudamore from Hempsted; the Duke of Norfolk's house in Westgate Street has only recently been demolished much to the chagrin of all conservationists, not least the Society for the Protection of Ancient Buildings which even offered to buy it. In 1789 the Duke chose his nephew Henry Howard of Thornbury Castle to stand for Barrow's seat. Opposing him was John Pitt, collector of Customs at the port, who sided with the local Blues, as Gloucester Tories called themselves, and who was Gloucester's largest private landlord (remembered now in Pitt Street). Pitt emerged the victor by one vote. Gloucester Tories formed a True Blue Club in honour of Pitt's victory. There were no more contests till 1805 when Pitt died.

One candidate was Lord Arthur Somerset, a nephew of the sixth Duke of Beaufort. The Duke, long a power in Gloucestershire county politics, was making his first and by no means his last attempt to extend his influence into the city. Somerset's agent was the Beaufort solicitor in Gloucester, Thomas Davis, who was the most active Tory in the city. The other candidate was Captain Robert Morris, the founder of the Royal Gloucester Yeomanry Cavalry. Morris was independent and because he was a local man and not blatantly Blue, enjoyed the support of the Corporation, and he won. He died in 1816, and this time the Corporation adopted an official candidate in Edward Webb, son of the former M.P. and brother-in-law to Sir Berkeley William Guise of Highnam, who represented the County in Parliament. Webb was supported by the newly organized Whig Club, founded expressly to combat the wealth and power of the Duke of Beaufort. The most important member of the Whig Club was Colonel William Fitzhardinge Berkeley, later Lord Segrave and Earl Fitzhardinge. Webb defeated the Beaufort candidate in 1816, but in the General Election of 1818, the honours were shared, the two successful candidates being Webb and the Beaufort nominee, R.B. Cooper. The expenses to the Berkeley and Beaufort families were enormous.

In June 1826 Parliament was dissolved and the country was stirred by the battle-cries calling for the repeal of the Corn Laws and for Roman Catholic emancipation. In Gloucester Cooper opposed both, while Webb called for reduction in taxes and parliamentary reform. King George IV died on 20 June 1830, causing another election, producing the first Whig ministry in a generation, and eventually the first political reform bill. At this election John Phillpotts, son of the landlord of the Bell Hotel, ousted Cooper. Of the three candidates he was the only one who lived in Gloucester, a confidential friend of the banker Jemmy Wood, and an original subscriber to the Gloucester-Berkeley canal.

In the 1831 election in the city all three candidates favoured reform; Webb, Phillpotts and Captain Maurice Frederick Berkeley. The Whig problem was complicated by the Berkeley family's engagement in county politics on behalf of Henry Moreton (later second Earl of Ducie) and Sir Berkeley William Guise who opposed Lord Edward Somerset in East Gloucestershire, and Berkeley finances had to be stretched to meet the cost of both elections. However, Captain Berkeley headed the poll in Gloucester and Phillpotts came last, losing his seat. In the pre-reform era the Gloucester voters did not change their minds about reform; but they did respond to financial inducement.

This was the political background to the Tory Francis Witts's diary.

The Diary
of a
Cotswold Parson

January 3rd, 1820

Left Upper Slaughter for Bath in the hope that another course of the waters may essentially strengthen my dear wife's constitution. Having sent forward my manservant and horse we travelled post with Edward and a maid. The weather very cold, frost and snow; more of the latter between home and Cirencester and between Petty France and Bath, than between Cirencester and Petty France. The roads very slippery and though a horse fell in the chaise in the streets of Tetbury, we providentially escaped any accident.

February 26th, 1820

Completed my 36th year. I give God thanks for His great mercies to me and mine, humbly praying for His aid to correct my many failings, and beseeching His protection in future.

March 2nd, 1820

My dear son Edward's 7th birthday. May the Almighty give strength to the powers both of his mind and body and may his parents train him up in the ways of religion and in useful learning.

May 12th, 1820

At Stow Fair this day Mr. Large of Broadwell, Oxfordshire, an eminent agriculturist, whose assistance I had called in as Land Surveyor here and at Stanway, pointed my attention to a sheep

Mrs Backhouse

bred by him and killed by a butcher of the place. Its size was indeed enormous as it weighed 69 lbs. to the quarter: the shoulder 35 lbs and so on in proportion; nothing could be more healthy than the whole appearance of the sheep, it was a three shear sheep, I believe of the mixed Cotswold and Lincolnshire breed. Mr. Large is remarkable for the size and small bones and fine wool of his sheep and makes large sums by the letting and sale of his rams.

July 5th, 1820

We passed the evening at Mr. Hippisley's retreat as he calls a summer house situate in his plantations at the foot of Stow Hill. No wonder that the more than octogenarian owner delights in these groves of his own plantation and rearing, laid out with simple and judicious taste.[1] Music added to the zest of the rural fete.

August 21st, 1820

We left home on a tour, with Mrs. Backhouse,[2] who wished by the way to look for a house for her future residence at Gloucester. Her carriage and horses were our mode of conveyance and soon brought us to Frogmill, 10 miles distance, where we baited, and in two hours reached Gloucester, 12 miles further. We went to the King's Head Inn: looked round the town, the spa[3] and its new buildings, visited the County Hall and Gaol. At the latter I had an interview with Joseph Palmer, a sheep stealer, whom I had committed and who had been tried, sentenced and left for execution. Though found guilty on the clearest and most direct evidence, this hardened young man, persisted in denying his crime, at the same time that he had every reason to believe that he would be hanged on the following Saturday: nor did my admonitions appear to affect him more than other exhortations which had been addressed to him.

1 E of the Foss Way was a romantic pleasure garden of c. 1800 with a wooded walk, passing under the road from Maugersbury by the Foss through a tunnel, and down to St. Edward's well. D. Verey, *Buildings of England, Gloucestershire: the Cotswolds.* 1970
2 Jane, née Moorhouse of Giggleswick, the mother of Margaret Witts.
3 Spa Road is more like Cheltenham than Gloucester. Maitland House has a Neo-Greek porch with fluted Greek Doric columns. Sherborne House and the Judges' Lodgings have splendid classical facades overlooking a miniature park. Gloucester, till c.1820, was the social centre; but after that it was quickly overtaken by the upstart Cheltenham.

Highnam, the seat of Sir B.W. Guise

August 26th, 1820

We looked into the Cathedral, where some alterations are going on under the auspices of Dr. Griffith, Prebendary, and Master of University College, whose taste in architecture and painting is generally known: as also his admirable work on wood, called poker painting, by which he produces portraits almost rivalling colours in delicacy of light and shade, and truth of expression. After luncheon we set off for Ross, crossing the Severn by a very handsome new bridge of a single arch, in the construction of which great skill and science have been displayed. Having left the paved causeway we came on a delightful level road, and passed on the right Highnam, the seat of Sir B.W. Guise,[1] one of the representatives of the county but not his residence, as he generally lives, when in the county, at Rendcomb near Cirencester. The country is very fertile and rich, partly meadow and partly corn land. The view of Gloucester Cathedral and the eminences skirting the vale and forming the ascent of the Cotswold country is very beautiful ... in front, May Hill, a conspicuous round topped hill distinguished by a plantation on the summit.[2] To the left in the direction of Blaisdon and Mitcheldean are fine masses of wood, sweeping along the hills, in the bosom of which is situated the pretty village of Longhope, with its spire: the preferment, I believe, belongs to Mr. Probyn, Archdeacon of Llandaff. Spires, indeed, prevail in this district, as at Lea, the last village in Gloucestershire .... The clerk who showed us Ross church, pointed to a simple machine used in the Civil war for laming cavalry horses; being pieces of iron, with three points, thrown in the roads by which the enemy was likely to pass. They were called Cats.

Among these ancient tombs is a modern pedestal and bust, admirably executed by Theed, the sculptor, being the tribute of his friends and neighbours to the late Mr. Westfaling, who died possessed of the Rudhall property, which had devolved to an heiress whose name on his marriage he assumed; his paternal name was Brereton, the son of a Gloucestershire clergyman.

Having returned to our Inn, to tea, the newspapers of the day claimed our attention, being the first of a series of horrible developments of the imputed adulteries and gross indecencies of the Queen Caroline. The examination of witnesses in support of the bill of pains and penalties is likely to last a considerable time, and

1 Sir Berkeley William Guise
2 So much for those who say it only dates from Queen Victoria's Jubilee.

satiate the country with the narrative of profligate amours and abandoned favourites.

April 27, 1821

The overseer of Halling brought up two gipsies, casual poor in their parish in order to their being examined to their settlement. Merach Lock the husband swore that he was born under an oak on Halling down as he had heard from his mother, being an illegitimate child and knowing nothing of his father: also that he was recently married to his wife Mary with whom he had cohabited twenty years, having by her six children. It seems that the Parish of Halling has little or no chance of proving him settled elsewhere. On examining the woman, she swore all the children to be Merach Lock's — Lucas and Adam being born like their father in the Parish of Halling — Eve at Cold Ashton — Sarah at Brimpsfield — Temperance at Hawkesbury — Joanna at Cranham.

The law was strictly interpreted and removal orders were made in respect of the last four children, sending them to their respective birth places.[1]

November 20th, 1822

My young friend and curate at Stanway,[2] Frederick Aston, accompanied by his college friend Walter Calverley Trevelyan,[3] left us after passing two days with us.

1 There are numerous examples of the making of removal orders in the diaries. Perhaps the harshest was heard at Northleach concerning this family. The orders were upheld following an appeal by the parishes of Hawkesbury and Cranham at the Trinity Quarter Sessions of 1821, which Witts himself attended.

2 Stanway was originally part of the endowment of Tewkesbury Abbey. In 1533 it was leased to Richard Tracy of Toddington. By 1678 the manor was owned by Ferdinando Tracy, younger son of John, Viscount Tracy of Rathcoole. In 1767 the manor passed to Henrietta, Viscountess Hereford, daughter of Anthony Tracy. She died in 1817, and was succeeded by her sister Susan, Lady Elcho, the mother of Francis Charteris, Earl of Wemyss. Lady Elcho was a cousin of Francis Witts's mother.

3 Son of Sir John Trevelyan of Wallington Hall, Northumberland.

December 14th, 1822

Yesterday I went to Stanway, dined and slept at the Vicarage with my friend Frederick Aston. The object of my visit was to distribute among the poor of the parish £36 in clothing and coal, and money which had been entrusted by Lady Elcho to my award. We gave 454 yards of linen, 10 tons of coal and £2.10.6 in money to the oldest persons in the several hamlets of Church Stanway, Wood Stanway, Taddington and Hornsleasow.

December 20th, 1822

I went yesterday to Cheltenham to meet our dear Edward on his return from school for the Christmas holidays. He arrived in a Bath coach in perfect health and spirits, the same engaging affectionate child as ever. We dined and slept at my Mother's in Belle Vue Place. Frederick Aston was also at Cheltenham on his way to Gloucester, to be examined for ordination; on Sunday he expects to be ordained priest.

We called this morning on my aunt, Mrs. Travell, whom we found in good health considering her very advanced age. Her present guest is my amiable and agreeable cousin Miss Buxton, granddaughter to my uncle and predecessor in this living, Mr. Ferdinando Tracy Travell. Miss Buxton, together with her brother-in-law Mr. F. Whalley and her cousin Mr. Naper,[1] has lately discharged an act of duty and affection to the memory of their deceased grandfather by causing to be erected in the chancel of my church a very elegant monument, designed by Mr. Naper himself and executed by Mr. C. Rossi, the sculptor, at an expense exceeding I believe £150. In order to represent the character of a pious parish priest Mr. Naper has combined in his design the emblems of the beginning and finishing sacraments with the liturgy. On a background of black marble is sculptured in statuary marble in high relief a Gothic front resting on a tablet; on the font rests the book of Common Prayer, and on the book the paten and chalice: The Tablet is inscribed: "Sacred to the memory of The Reverend F.T. Travell, M.A. who died on the 27th day of September 1808 in the 69th year of his age, having been 45 years Rector of this Parish." Rossi had before executed in the church at Stow a beautiful monument to Mrs. Hippisley, wife of my worthy old friend the late Rector of that Parish.

December 31st, 1822

At the close of the year I have to mention the enlargement of the church at Upper Slaughter, which has been to me a source of much anxiety, and the completion, as is the case with all sublunary concerns, has in some measure disappointed the hopes with which I engaged in the work. The increased population of the parish, and still more of the appendant extraparochial place, Eyford, required additional church accommodation, and the proprietor of Eyford, Mr. V. Dolphin[1] had for some time voluntarily offered to be at the expense, when he should come of age. Towards the close of last year he expressed his desire that the work should begin, and said that he destined £300 to its completion, and pointed out his ideas on the mode of doing the work, namely by taking down the ancient (Norman) diminutive north aisle, and erecting in its stead an aisle as large as the nave. The parish met him by engaging to erect a gallery across the new erection. The work under my direction was executed in the course of the summer. Increased room for more than 70 persons was gained. Mr. Dolphin was accommodated in the body of the church with excellent pews for himself and his domestics, having before been only by sufferance admitted into the pews in the chancel. When finished an increase of expenditure had been incurred above the estimate allotted to Mr. Dolphin, and that allotted to the parish. That gentleman had never once expressed an intention of limiting himself to the estimate of £230. The whole expense now exceeded £400 and Mr. Dolphin paid only £230.[2] From November 1st to this date neither Mr. Dolphin nor myself have exchanged a word. My uneasiness arising out of these disputes has been very great.

January 8th, 1823

Dined at Oddington with Lady Reade[3] and Sir John. The usual showy display, and well-lighted cheer. How foolish it is to set out for a dinner party in the country after dark, and drive seven miles.

1 There are frequent references to Mr. & Mrs. Dolphin in the diaries. His extravagances caused his wife much embarrassment. Generally the story of the Dolphins has been omitted.
2 See 'History of St. Peter's Church, Upper Slaughter', by Dennis Corble.
3 Oddington House was re-modelled and enlarged c.1810 for Lady Reade.

January, 10th, 1823

Attended the quarterly Petty Sessions at Northleach Bridewell, after which I went on to dine and sleep at Mr. Price's, the Rector of Coln St. Dennis. Met there a Mr. Lee, a Roman Catholic priest, residing at Hatherop where he has a chapel. Sir John Webb formerly possessor of Hatherop estate was a Roman Catholic. The present owner is Mr. Ponsonby whose wife, Lady Barbara Ashley,[1] is granddaughter and heiress of Sir John and daughter of the late Earl of Shaftesbury.

January 11th, 1823

Attended a meeting at Northleach convened to support a projected bridge over the Severn at Haw Passage between Gloucester and Tewkesbury, intended to shorten the communication between Hereford and London, through Cheltenham. Lord Sherborne presided and it was reported that nearly as much money was subscribed as was required: the estimate being £24,000 and £21,000 subscribed. A rival company of projectors also advocate a bridge at the Mythe near Tewkesbury, to cross the Severn above its junction with the Avon ... and it is affirmed that the route to the metropolis through Stow would be shorter and preferable. Ample funds are subscribed for their project and it seems that each party will carry their views into effect.

January, 14th, 1823

The Sessions (in Gloucester) commenced. The bench was very crowded. The Lord Lieutenant, Lord Apsley, M.P. for Cirencester, Mr. Pitt, M.P. for Cricklade ...

January 18th, 1823

The Sessions will close this day. I returned home by Cheltenham to be ready for the duties of my churches.

---

1 Barbara, Lady de Mauley, died 1844. Her mortuary chapel at Hatherop Church was designed by   William Burges.

January 20th, 1823
　　I returned to Gloucester by Cheltenham on horseback.

January 21st, 1823
　　Looked into the new Church[1] at the Spa, now nearly finished. It is intended for the accommodation of the inhabitants of the new town, which within these few years has arised round the saline springs and forms a genteel suburb to the city. It is extraparochial, and the church under the auspices of the Bishop is erected by subscription. The edifice is slight, and erected, I should presume at no very great expense; the interior will be commodious and well-lighted.

January 24th, 1823
　　Rode through the villages of Tuffley, Whaddon and Brook-thorp. This is a new but very bad turnpike road to Stroud, winding round the foot of Robins Wood Hill amid rich enclosures, which in summer would afford pleasing landscapes. You survey the magnificent Vale of the Severn from the Malvern Hills to below Newnham, the former tipped with snow and showing their waving outline to advantage against the leaden coloured sky. May Hill contrasts well with the long and silvery reaches of the Severn; the village towers afford resting points to the eye in the flat part of the landscape. Gloucester with its Cathedral and towers appeared to much advantage as I returned.

January 25th, 1823
　　I returned home by Cheltenham. Snow came on as I left, with a keen east wind, as I rode, meeting me; it was with difficulty I could see my way and the front of my horse as well as my own face were coated with ice when I reached Upper Slaughter.

January 28th, 1823
　　The severity of the weather having prevented my return to Gloucester yesterday, I returned thither to-day. A thaw has come

---

1 Christ Church, Brunswick Road, Gloucester, by Rickman & Hutchinson, 1822.

on; but I found the riding difficult from the remains of snow on the hills, and flood between Cheltenham and Gloucester. Learnt the news of the sudden death of the eminent Dr. Jenner,[1] the discoverer of vaccination, which happened at Berkeley on the 26th. Apoplexy was the malady which quickly terminated his useful life at the age of 74.

February 12th, 1823

It is announced that Mr. Vansittart is appointed Chancellor of the Duchy of Lancaster in the room of C.B. Bathurst of Lydney Park, Chairman of our Quarter Sessions.

February 17th, 1823

Mrs. Cooke, an intimate friend of my mother spent the evening with us. She is widow of the brave Captain Cooke of the Bellerophon, who was killed in the Battle of Trafalgar.[2]

April 24th, 1823

Proceeded to Bourton-on-the-Hill where I dined and slept night at Dr. Warneford's,[3] meeting only Mr. Large of Broadwell, Oxfordshire, an eminent land surveyor who is engaged in laying out Dr. Warneford's rectorial allotments, under the new inclosure of the parish, having been employed by Dr. W. to protect his interests during the progress of the Act.

---

1 Edward Jenner (1749-1823). Began to practise at Berkeley in 1773. First vaccinated from cow-pox, 1796. Vaccination was made compulsory in England in 1853. Statues of Jenner are in Kensington gardens, Gloucester Cathedral, and at Boulogne and Brünn.

2 Capt. John Cooke (1763-1805). Put on shore by the Spithead mutineers, 1797.

3 Dr. Warneford was a very well-known benefactor of charities in Gloucestershire and elsewhere. The Warneford Diocesan and Ecclesiastical Charities had in 1855 as their first trustees, the Bishop of Gloucester and Bristol; the Very Revd. the Hon. Edward Rice, Dean of Gloucester; the Venerable John Timbrill, Archdeacon of Gloucester; Lord Redesdale of Batsford; William Dickins; John Curtis Hayward of Quedgeley; and Allen Alexander Bathurst of Oakley Park, Cirencester. The clerical trustees remain to this day the holders of the above offices, and there are two acting lay trustees and two nominating lay trustees.

July 15th, 1823

Mr. Bathurst's (Rt. Hon. C. Bragge Bathurst) seat in Gloucestershire is at Lydney in the Forest of Dean. He has probably finally quitted public life as he is now no longer a Member of Parliament and Chancellor of the Duchy of Lancaster. He was bred to the law, was a hard-working politician, but not a man of great parts, prolix in parliament, a frequent speaker but no orator. His connexion with Lord Sidmouth, which was by marriage, principally contributed to bringing him forward.

September 16th, 1823

I rode down to Gloucester, where my dear wife had arrived the evening before on a visit to Mrs. Backhouse. The town was alive with the approaching festivity of the Triennial Music Meeting.

September 17th, 1823

At an early hour we repaired to the Cathedral where service was to be performed, with sacred music and a sermon preached before a collection for the widows and orphans of the distressed clergy of the three dioceses of Gloucester, Worcester and Hereford. This is the hundredth anniversary of this excellent charity.[1] The lay stewards on the present occasion are Mr. Estcourt, M.P. for Devizes, of Estcourt House, near Tetbury, Chandos Leigh [2] of Adlestrop, and Mr. Goodrich, resident at Wotton in the immediate vicinity of Gloucester.

Chandos Leigh is an eccentric mortal, possessed of talent and studious in an odd way. He has been a warm admirer of theatrical performances and performers, male and female; a poet in a small way; one of his earlier productions, "the Pleasures of Love" was, by the prudence of his friends, suppressed. He resides much at Adlestrop but without taking a share in the public business of the county and neighbourhood. The clerical stewards are Dr. Timbrill, rector of Beckford, a strong headed, intelligent, active man, a

1 The 250th. Three Choirs Festival was held in Gloucester in 1977. It started in about 1715 as a gathering of musical clubs in Hereford, Worcester and Gloucester. With a few years it was well established, and must be one of the oldest music meetings in Europe.
2 Chandos Leigh, born 1792; gained favourable reputation as a poet; created Baron Leigh, of Stoneleigh, 1839.

leading magistrate in this county and Treasurer of the Clergy Charity, Mr. Selwyn, a Prebendary of Gloucester, and the Reverend Wadham Huntley, rector of Eastington and Aston Blank.

We obtained very good seats in the choir, and the whole of the Cathedral was extremely crowded. The orchestra is erected in front of the Organ facing the altar; the area between the pulpit and altar filled with benches, the space occupied by the altar is covered by raised sittings, one behind another in ranges, up to the top of the screen, and to-day, there were arranged here various schools, the young ladies of each being dressed uniformly, which was a very pretty sight. On each side of the inner choir, the large arches above the stalls, opening into the transepts were filled with temporary galleries, that on the right being appropriated to the friends of the lay stewards, that on the left to those of the clerical stewards. These galleries being almost wholly filled with ladies in elegant morning dresses present a most beautiful parterre to the eye. Indeed, the spectacle, especially on these mornings, the second and third, when the admission is not free, is peculiarly brilliant. Not any other ecclesiastical building in the Kingdom, I believe, is better adapted for sacred music on a grand scale, and the united charms of solemn strains and exquisite architecture impress the mind in the most striking manner. The Dettinger Te Deum, the Overture to Esther, Dr. Boyce's Anthem (Charity) and Knyvett's new Coronation anthem were the musical treats for the morning.

The Ordinary for Gentlemen is held alternately at the two principle Inns; this day it was at the King's Head. I dined there. Mr. Chandos Leigh was in the Chair. I sat agreeably between Dr. Cooke, the Chairman of the Quarter Sessions and Mr. Baker of Hardwicke Court. The party was very numerous, I should think more than 70 sat down, and among them the leading persons in the county.

I joined my wife in the noble room in the Shire Hall, which serves for County meetings, and on this occasion for concerts and balls. We obtained very good seats, and the selection of music was very judicious. Tea and a ball followed the concert, for neither of which we remained, being anxious to husband Margaret's strength for the ensuing days. Very numerous and large parties resorted from Cheltenham.

September 19th, 1823

We went to the Oratorio in the Cathedral the *Messiah,* which was equally well attended as the *Redemption* yesterday. Nothing could be more magnificent or a finer treatment in music than the performance this day. The eye was equally delighted, and to me the assembly of so many acquaintance as I now number in the County, was an additional relish. The Collections at the doors of the Cathedral on the three days have amounted to £759.14.5., nearly as large as the largest collection ever made.

September 20th, 1823

I attended a meeting of the subscribers to a monument in memory of Sir G.O. Paul.[1] This languishing testimony of gratitude for public services is now at last likely to be carried into effect. Mr. Cripps, M.P. the Chairman, produced sketches by Flaxman for the consideration of the meeting, which consisted of a few leading magistrates. A monument of statuary marble 4ft 7½ in. high and 9 ft in length, to be erected in the Cathedral was most approved, including two figures on each side of the tablet in height 3'4'' of Wisdom and Justice: on the whole an elegant design.

I rode home for my Sunday's duty in the afternoon.

September 22nd, 1823

In the afternoon I rode to Northleach to meet the *Regulator* Coach on its return to Gloucester from London by which I rejoined my family in Wellington Parade.

October 11th, 1823

After calling at Stanway House, where I remained till after luncheon ... passed near Toddington where the magnificent Gothic mansion of Mr. Hanbury Tracy,[2] the exterior of which is now completed, presents a very handsome object from the road. Mr.

[1] Sir George Onesiphorus (philanthropist), son of Sir Onesiphorus Paul, cloth manufacturer in Woodchester where George was born in 1746. High Sheriff, 1780. The County Gaol was rebuilt at his instigation and from his designs, and new prisons were built at Horsley, Lawford's Gate, Littledean and Northleach under his supervision. He died in 1820 and was buried in Gloucester Cathedral.

[2] The Hanbury family owned the Pontypool Ironworks. Charles Hanbury was born in 1778, and married in 1798 Henrietta daughter and heiress of the 8th Viscount Tracy of Rathcoole, taking the additional name of Tracy. In 1838 he was created Baron Sudeley of Toddington.

Tracy has combined in this structure, with much judgement and taste, and at very great expense, some of the most interesting *morceaux* of ancient gothic architecture from Oxford and other places. A tower rises in the centre copied from that of Magdalen College, and the cloister and grand entrance of the same college are imitated in the principal front of the mansion; the west window of Tintern Abbey appears in miniature in what is called a chapel return; but in fact is not a chapel, the interior being laid out in domestic apartments. The remains of the old mansion of the Lords Tracy not far distant from the new house, still afford a residence to the family, while the more splendid edifice is in progress towards completion.

Sunday October 12th, 1823

I had been appointed to preach the Anniversary Sermon for the Tewkesbury dispensary in the venerable Abbey Church. The massive Norman columns, the fine western round headed window, the solid massive tower, the interesting ancient monuments, covering the remains of many princes, nobles and warriors, all deserve to be examined at leisure. The inner choir has been fitted up for divine service several years ago at considerable expense, and with judgement except as to the pulpit where the attempt to produce Gothic symmetry and lightness has ended in a very gingerbread sort of rostrum, and to the preacher a most uncomfortable, and at first view, insecure pulpit. The congregation was not large but very respectable. The Corporation in their robes occupied the seat appropriated to them. I met with great politeness, and the collection exceeded my expectations, amounting to nearly £24. In the church I saw an old mural monument to the memory of the wife of one of the Slaughters, an old family who long held the manor of Upper Slaughter and resided in the ancient mansion house of my village, at present occupied by a tenant of Lord Sherborne, who is the present Lord of the Manor of Upper Slaughter.

October 14th, 1823

The Quarter Sessions began. The business was not so great as usual. It is gratifying to find a diminution of crime everywhere both as to the number and heinousness of offences. The Duke of Beaufort attended. The number of magistrates dining together on the first three days of the Session at the King's Head, was rather less than is common. This custom of dining together and passing the evening in each other's company tends much to maintain that friendly harmony and mutual good intelligence which distinguishes the Gloucestershire Sessions.

October 21st, 1823

I attended a meeting of the Trustees of the Gloucestershire District of the Crickley Hill Turnpike road. It is now in agitation to avoid Dowdeswell hill, a steep and dangerous declivity by a deviation winding gently up the valley behind the Parsonage, passing between Sandywell Park and the village of Whittington. The trustees dined together at the King's Head, Lord Sherborne presided.

October 24th, 1823

Stow Fair. Renewed hopes of letting my rectorial farm.

October 25th, 1823

Agreed with Mr. John Davis, now tenant to Mr. Commeline, rector of Cowley, for the occupation of my rectorial farm at the low rent of £140 per annum, about 13/- per acre on an average of green land and arable. I am moreover to find him a house or build one by midsummer.

October 30th, 1823

My mother arrived from Stanway. The party there is broken up and Lady Elcho goes to London. After a day of severe rain, with a cold wind, the evening and night were very tempestuous, with sleet, snow and rain.

October 31st, 1823

On rising this morning we were informed of the devastations of the storm last night. In our pleasure ground we have lost a very fine stately elm, the pride of the lawn, blown down without committing any injury. In the shady walk four or five fine elms have been uprooted. In the orchard a very handsome and productive spreading apple tree, besides smaller trees and limbs scattered in all directions over the grounds.

December 23rd, 1823

After breakfast I left Stanway in a post chaise, for which I had sent from Broadway and reached Cheltenham by 1.30. The road to Winchcombe is better than it used to be, and a great alteration has been made between Winchcombe and Southam by which the road is carried round the tremendous hill, which is formerly ascended only to sink again into the vale by a precipitous descent. By thus skirting Cleeve Cloud there is no very heavy draught.

March 31st, 1824

I proceeded to Gloucester. The forenoon was mostly taken up by me in seeing servants of different descriptions enquiring for places in our family, a quarrel in our kitchen having caused us to dismiss most of our domestics.

The Commission of Assize for the County was opened this afternoon. The new High Sheriff is my friend Thomas John Lloyd-Baker, of Hardwicke Court, a very worthy, intelligent country gentleman and magistrate whose deserved popularity was sufficiently evinced by the very numerous party upwards of 70 gentlemen who dined with him. The hilarity of the evening was, however, exchanged for a strong feeling of gloom by a melancholy accident, which be-fell Mr. Winchomb Hicks of Eastington, an eminent young clothier, and esteemed magistrate, as he was setting out to ride home about 9 o'clock. Though he appeared quite sober when he left the party, the outward air had the effect of making him very unsteady, insomuch that he was found on the Bristol road, a little beyond the Spa, fallen from his horse and almost dead.

April 20th, 1824

The Duke of Wellington is now in Cheltenham for the benefit of his health. I saw him to-day for the first time. He was walking with my acquaintance, Lord Apsley, eldest son of Earl Bathurst. The great Captain of the Age is much attached to this agreeable young nobleman. The Duke's countenance is very striking; but carries with it the appearance of a great wear and tear of constitution.

Bowden Hall the seat of James Byles

April 22nd, 1824

Walked to the village of Charlton Kings. Since I have been in the interior of this pretty village several nice villas and genteel cottages have been added to it. The church is undergoing a complete repair; enlarged accommodation and galleries being provided, with new pews: the whole will be very neat.

April 24th, 1824

Leaving my wife at Cheltenham, I returned home to perform my duty. On my way to Upper Slaughter I explored the new line of road marked out, to avoid Dowdeswell Hill, which, diverging to the left at the foot of the hill, winds up the valley towards Whittington. Where it approaches Sandywell Park there will be a cutting of 30 ft. Running between Whittington Court and Sandywell Park it crosses the Stow road at Andoversford and comes into the original road to Northleach a little above Frogmill Inn. It will be a great relief to travelling and lead through a pleasing line of country.

Mr. Lawrence, Mrs. Lightbourne's heir, has not been idle since the old lady's decease. He is about to make Sandywell Park his residence and is employing many people there in altering and modernizing the house, in enlarging the Park as far as the new line of road, and in planting. It is said that he is about to marry some rich heiress.

April 30th, 1824

I visited the Lunatic Asylum, going over every part of it with the resident medical man. The institution is under the direction of a committee of visiting magistrates and subscribers, of whom my acquaintance, the intelligent and assiduous Mr. Byles,[1] of Bowden Hall near Gloucester, a very active and able magistrate, is the main stay.

May 6th, 1824

At a meeting of the Commissioners of the Foss and Cross Turnpike roads, the engineer of the Stratford and Moreton-in-

1 James H. Byles. Bowden Hall was afterwards occupied by the Birchall family.

Marsh railway communicated much information on the subject of rail roads, either in progress or in agitation. The Stratford railroad will be completed in December next. £146,000 have recently been subscribed to form a railway between Liverpool and Birmingham. From Moreton-in-Marsh a railroad is projected by the valley of the Evenlode through Wychwood Forest, by Cassington to Oxford. Another railway diverging at Oddington and proceeding to Idbury is meant to cross the country to Latton near Cricklade, there to join the North Wilts Canal and so extend a line to Bristol. These are sanguine schemes but in the present redundance of capital, funds for the execution may be found, and they are more deserving of support than Columbian or Peruvian or Mexican loans, or than many other bubbles of this stock-jobbing age. Besides, the power of steam, and the new discoveries in science and mechanics, render easy and cheap schemes, which even a few years since would have been considered hopeless. The tram waggons now may be made to travel without horses by steam, and are so worked both in Yorkshire and Northumberland.

July 13th, 1824

The lingering affair of the monument to Sir G.O. Paul was again brought forward. It is now proposed to employ a rising young artist, by name Sievier, who is to execute the monument in memory of Dr. Jenner, now in progress and also to be erected by subscription. The difficulty of making a good resemblance of Sir G. Paul is great. The only guide Mr. Sievier had to follow was a small medallion in wax, the production of Lady Denbigh, Lord Ducie's daughter many years ago, and Mr. Seivier's bust was not a likeness of Sir G. Paul. This will however be remedied in another attempt. The Rev. C. Crawley has forwarded from memory a sketch, which in the principal features is a great resemblance, and which he has given to Mr. Sievier as an aid for the modelling of his bust. (It proved useless.) The rest of the monument is proposed to consist of a tablet with an emblematical figure and drapery, to be erected in the Cathedral.

My aunt Lady Lyttelton having left my wife at Upper Slaughter, after being a guest at Stow, the seat of the Duke of Buckingham for the christening of the Marquis of Chandos's eldest son, arrived at Gloucester to-day to visit my cousins Anne and Apphia Witts who still remain here in lodgings at the Spa, where Mrs. Backhouse and myself also passed part of the evening.

July 29th, 1824

Frederick Aston, my curate at Stanway, arrived to communicate a very distressing event which had happened at Stanway this morning, the suicide of one of the parishioners, a married woman of the name of Kendrick, about sixty years of age, who drowned herself in the canal, a piece of water in the pleasure grounds of Stanway House. Kendrick, the husband is committed to gaol for refusing to answer questions put to him by the Commissioners of his bankruptcy (as an innkeeper at Toddington.) The want of sound religious principle, uncontrolled passionateness of feeling, and dread of poverty and accumulated distress have no doubt brought on the temporary insanity, under the influence of which the wretched woman has sought a watery grave.

August 15th, 1824

I exchanged duties with Frederick Aston, and dined and slept at Wood Stanway. Recent irregularities at Stanway ending in the birth of three illegitimate children, seemed to require animadversion from the pulpit, which they accordingly received from the Vicar.

September 10th, 1824

Our old friend Mr. Wellford came on a visit. He was curate at Moreton-in-Marsh, Dr. Warneford having engaged him. But with very delicate health and a mind not greatly attuned to cheerfulness, accustomed also not to look on the bright side of things, he had imbibed and encouraged in himself many of those religious views, which mark the class known by the name of Evangelical, being devoid, however, of many of the weak characteristics of that party, ostentation, cant and uncharitableness. This cast, as it developed itself, proved very disagreeable to Dr. Warneford, who plumed himself on his high church principles, and a separation between the Rector and curate ensued, which required some delicacy of management and at which I was present.

November 1st, 1824

I went to Stanway by Lady Elcho's invitation to meet some of her neighbours at dinner.

In the forenoon I went to Wood Stanway, called at the Vicarage, and overlooked some building on the farm, which is now nearly completed. It consists of commodious feeding stalls for twelve oxen. Since I have had the living, I have spent several hundred pounds in fencing, building and draining.

Sir Thomas and Lady Phillipps [1] from Middle Hill, Mr. and Mrs. Gist, two Miss Gists and Mr. W. Gist joined the dinner party. Sir Thomas was lately created a Baronet. He cannot boast of being an hereditary gentleman; his father raised himself from menial employments to considerable wealth by successful enterprise in the most money-making times of the cotton manufactory. He retired to his native parish, Broadway, and the Baronet is the offspring of an illegitimate union. The lady has no greater pretensions to legitimacy, and is a boisterous dame strongly contrasting with his reserve. He is an antiquary, book collector, who has yet perhaps still more experience to buy than he has yet paid for, but report says much trash has already been foisted upon him.

Mr. Gist is the eldest son of the rich parvenue residing at Wormington Grange, and has recently been married to Mary Anne Westenra, daughter of Lord Rossmore, but possessing neither talent nor beauty. The acquaintance was formed at Stanway in the autumn of last year fostered by the able diplomacy of my cousin Augusta of Rossmore.

November 6th, 1824

Mrs. Backhouse left us to return to Gloucester. We shall regret her absence, so sensible a person is she, and so judicious, so well principled, and so warmly attached to Margaret and myself and her grandson. I cannot speak too highly of her openness and liberality in all money matters.

December 20th, 1824

I walked to Wormington Grange (from Stanway) to call on the Gist family. These estimable people had been very kind to my mother, who had visited them for a fortnight during a recent absence of Lady Elcho in town. It is a comfortable but not a handsome place. The younger Mr. Gist has a small museum of

---

1 Sir Thomas Phillipps (1792-1872) made one of the greatest collections of books and manuscripts ever gathered together, one which has still been appearing in the sale rooms to this day. Created baronet, 1821. Established private printing press at Middle Hill. Later, moved to Thirlestane House, Cheltenham.

natural curiosities, serpents, birds, insects, fossils, etc. with a few articles of dress from the South Sea Islands, which afforded great amusement to my dear boy.

Miss Gist, whose solicitude for my mother is very great, successfully aided me in prevailing on her to quit Stanway House for her own home, No. 2 Belle Vue Place, Cheltenham.[1]

January 18th, 1825

My mother's funeral at Chipping Norton. A most gloomy wet morning after a stormy night was congenial to the depression of my spirits. It was half past ten before we could reach the church. The service was performed by the curate, a vulgar unfeeling man: his careless manner, his uncouth pronunciation and coarse appearance were all forbidding. Crowds of curious spectators flocked round the coffin and vault; but all was curiosity, no sympathy was visible; most trying is this appearance of indifference and equally so the suppressed voices of the assistants as they lowered the coffin through the narrow mouth of the vault, grating against the top of the arch and at length deposited beside the last inmate of the dark abode.

I cannot and ought not to lose sight of the blessings still reserved to me by a gracious Providence, an affectionate wife, a promising child, and ample provision of earthly comforts.

We returned to the mourning coach immediately after the funeral and reached Cheltenham at 7 p.m.

May 9th, 1825

We left home on a long talked of visit to my aunt Apphia[2] Lady Lyttelton at Malvern. We divided our first stage to Tewkesbury by baiting for an hour at Wood Stanway. At Tewkesbury we remained half an hour, where we sought and at last found, in a neat cottage, an estimable person, late a servant of Margaret's, Frances Hollis, her father is an excise man. We had a very awkward pair of horses to Malvern; the run on the road was unusual and we were the last

1 Here she died on January 9th. She was 76 having been born in 1748, Agnes, the daughter of John Travell of Swerford, Oxfordshire, her mother the daughter of John Tracy of Stanway.
2 Apphia, a Christian name often used in the Witts family, comes from St. Paul's epistle to Philemon.

travellers, so that an ill-assorted pair of animals, and without a regular boy, we went the first mile or two in a little alarm; but when we were all used to each other jogged on very comfortably to the end of the stage. As we walked over the bridges at the confluence of the Severn and Avon we greatly admired the sweet meadow verdure, and the diversity of cheerful objects presented to our view. Mythe Hill is much improved, and the neat villas on its summit greatly ornament the bank. At its foot are the abutments of the projected bridge [1] nearly in a state of completion, and ready for the iron arch to be thrown over the Severn; beyond is the straight road, marked out, but as yet not made, which will lead to Ledbury.

May 18th, 1825

Lady Lyttelton gave a *dejeuner à la fourchette* to her acquaintance. The day was very fine, and the company strolled in the garden or amused themselves in conversation in the drawing-room. The arrangements were very suitable; but it seemed unnecessary at 82 to undergo so much fatigue about the entertainment of persons, the majority of whom were mere strangers.

May 20th, 1825 Cheltenham

I took a walk to the site of Pittville, the projected new town to the north of the High Street and to the right hand of the Evesham Road, opposite to Marl Hill. The walks, which have been laid out and already planted, extend from the extremity of the town on the Prestbury road to the gentle eminence, on which the first stone of the proposed Pump room was lately laid with great masonic ceremony. This speculation will doubtless be lucrative to the first projector, Mr. Pitt, M.P. for Cricklade, whose estate will be parcelled out for the new erections, which on paper make an imposing appearance. How far the sub-projectors, builders etc. may profit will depend on the popularity of the situation. But the recent great extension of Cheltenham in every direction holds out to them also promising hopes. Mr. Pitt is one of those fortunate members of the legal profession, whom great sagacity, lucky opportunity and the skill of seizing on favourable circumstances

---

1 By Thomas Telford. Cast iron with a single span of 170 ft.

have elevated from a very humble to a very prosperous situation in life. His enterprises as attorney, banker, speculator in land and many other ways of gaining or losing fortunes, have been eminently successful. Cirencester was the scene where his prosperity was first laid, and he has been extremely lucky in his Cheltenham dealings.

Mr. Pitt's eldest son Cornelius, the Rector of Hazleton in this diocese, and curate of Chedworth, a contemporary of mine at Oxford and a worthy man and good magistrate, was so unfortunate as to forfeit his father's favour by marrying a widow Mrs. Robins, who had a family by her former husband, a connexion of Mr. Pitt's. It is expected the father will in so far relax from his animosity as to give him the living of Rendcomb which is in his gift, when it shall be vacant.

May 25th, 1825

From Broadway I rode along the beautiful valley below Middle Hill and crept up to the retired village of Snowshill, perched near the summit of the ridge sloping from the Cotswolds into the vale, a romantic little place. There is a good old-fashioned mansion house [1] where Mr. C. Marshall, Lord Wemyss's steward resides. It was the day of Broadway feast and I met many a cheerful healthy party of villagers trudging in pursuit of pleasure to the annual gala, enlivening the seclusion of this otherwise lonely vale. From Snowshill I proceeded across Cutsdean and Taddington hills, and by Kineton Thorns homewards.

June 10th, 1825

Mrs. Backhouse arrived from Gloucester to pass with Margaret the time she had yet to remain in Cheltenham. We all drank tea together at Mrs. Travell's, and walked in Sherborne Walks, which are grown up to be very shady and pleasant. This is not the fashionable well but there was a sprinkling of company and the evening delightful. The few musicians in the pump room played charmingly.

---

1 Snowshill Manor, now owned by the National Trust.

Prinknash Park the seat of Thomas Howell

June 13th, 1825

I left Cheltenham at about 2.30 o'clock. I set off by the Bath and Birmingham coach, being seated on the box. The day, as the preceding had been, was oppressively hot and scorching with no breath of air stirring. Our route was by Stroud and a new line through Painswick. It is a most strikingly beautiful drive ... fine beech woods clothing the steep knolls, with the road elegantly winding according to the conformation of the side of the hill. Well might the old King [1] exclaim, as it is said he did, surely a finer prospect cannot be seen within my dominions. Prinknash Park, the seat of my friend T. Howell, [2] is a pleasing object adjacent to the road. The venerable old-fashioned mansion, within which I have enjoyed the hospitality of its talented owner, resembles Stanway House in its arrangements and architecture, and like it was of ecclesiastical origin. Mr. Howell's father was editor of the *State Trials*, and the same valuable publication is continued by his son, who was like his father bred to the bar, at which however he does not practise; but at present holds the important situation of Judge Advocate at Gibraltar. While resident on his estate he was an ornament of the bench of magistrates, his legal acquirements being very extensive to which he adds considerable literary acquirements, with a great store of anecdote, and a felicity of expression which renders him a peculiarly agreeable companion.

At Castle Godwin, a small place perched among the beech woods contiguous to Painswick resides Mr. Lake formerly of Liverpool, an opulent merchant largely engaged in the silk trade. The situation of Painswick is delightful; this town is in the clothing district.

The living is valuable and in the gift of the inhabitant house-holders of all classes, even the poorest, and consequently elective. On a recent occasion the place presented all the intrigue, bustle and chicanery of a contested borough; legal assessors, counsel, and attorneys, bribery, bold swearing, clamour and warm excitement.

At Stroud we found a company of the 10th Hussars: these troops had been summoned a few days ago to assist the civil power in quelling a riotous uprising of the operative weavers. A certain degree of dissatisfaction has existed for some time about wages,

1 George III
2 Thomas Jones Howell was son of Thomas Bayly Howell, editor of the first 15 vols. of the 1808-18 edition of 'State Trials'.

which led to disorderly assemblages, actual violence, and alarming tumult.[1]

July 18th, 1825

We dined at Mr. Price's at Coln St. Dennis. The intense heat, the thermometer being at 90°, made this almost a service of danger. We had serious fears on the road, as the post horses in ascending the hills towards Northleach laboured most pitiously. There was a large party but everyone seemed languid and exhausted. We met Sir James Musgrave[2] of Barnsley Park, High Sheriff for the County.

July 19th, 1825

A still more oppresive, sultry and scorching day than yesterday.

1 Although the 18th and early 19th Century was a period of prosperity, long before 1825 the shrewder clothiers knew something was wrong. Profits were minimal and capital was tied up with threats of bankruptcy to follow. Cottage weavers suffered most of all.

2 Nobody during the whole of the nineteenth century, least of all Sir James Musgrave apparently, realized that hidden in his library was one of the most interesting lost collections of books in the world, Sir Isaac Newton's library.

In 1778, Sir James Musgrave, Bart., took the Newton books from Chinnor to Barnsley Park, which he had just inherited from his cousin Cassandra Perrot. For the next 140 years they were to lie there, even more lost sight of than they had been in Chinnor. He died in 1814 and was succeeded by his bachelor son another Sir James who reigned at Barnsley Park until 1858. He was the High Sheriff in 1825. The next baronet was his brother William Augustus, rector of Chinnor, described by his bishop as wholly irreligious; another brother Richard Adolphus, rector of Barnsley, had died in 1840. That the books finally came to light on the occasion of the Thame Park sale in 1920 was the result of an inter-county marriage in the 1830's, when Caroline Musgrave married Wenman Wykeham and the family eventually becoming the Wykeham-Musgraves of Thame Park Oxfordshire, and of Barnsley Park Gloucestershire, to which they succeeded on the death of William Augustus in 1875. Wenman Aubrey Wykeham-Musgrave, 1837-1915 was succeeded by Herbert Wenman Wykeham-Musgrave, 1871-1931.

Thame Park was put up for sale in 1920, and to help swell the books in the sale many of the Newton books were sent across from Barnsley Park. In bundles, some of 200 volumes, and reckoned by the auctioneer to be of little value, they were knocked down at give-away prices. Eventually, the world of learning was alerted. In the British Musem Library was found the original inventory of the 1,896 books sent down to Chinnor in 1728, but of these only 860 now remained at Barnsley Park. Through the generosity of an anonymous American these were purchased by the Pilgrim Trust and presented to Sir Isaac Newton's old Cambridge college — Trinity.

The thermometer stood in the shade at 92° and in the sun about 11 o'clock against the wall of Stanway House at 122°.[1]

November 9th, 1825

Mr. Sievier [2] is the sculptor employed to design and execute the two monuments now erecting in the Cathedral, to Sir G. Paul and Dr. Jenner. He was, I am told, bred up an engineer and has only of late turned his talents to the art of sculpture. He has obtained great credit for a celebrated bust of the Lord Chancellor, which he has most felicitously conceived, and has it in charge now to engage in some elaborate works of art, to be placed in the palace about to be erected on the site of Buckingham House. I found him a very unaffected, well-informed, agreeable man; his mind has not been exclusively applied to the study of the fine arts, as he seems by his conversation deeply versed in mechanics and chemistry. The Committee for the erection of the two monuments entrusted the execution to him partly because his anxiety to distinguish himself would tempt him to forego that large profit which Chantrey and other established sculptors of eminence insist upon. [3]

November 12th, 1825

Before leaving Gloucester, I went to the Cathedral to take a look at Sievier's monuments nearly completed. It cannot be called a correct resemblance of Jenner; but at any period of his life he was a very unsuitable study for a sculptor, the figure, broad, thickset, clumsy and the countenance coarse, though very intelligent when lighted up by the talent within.

December 15th, 1825

My friend and neighbour (at Oddington) Dr. Rice announced to us to-day his being nominated Dean of Gloucester, and received our congratulations. The vacancy arises from the recent death of Dr. Plumptre; the late Dean was a very respectable Divine,

---

1 Similar temperatures were reached in the summer of 1976.
2 Robert William Sievier (1794-1865). Exhibited in Royal Academy 1822-1844.
3 Sir Francis Chantrey (1781-1841) was paid three hundred guineas by George IV for his bust in 1822.

formerly private tutor to Earl Bathurst, by whose interest he obtained this preferment: he has suffered for many years from the stone.

January 13th, 1826

The business in hand at the Sessions, was the trial of several weavers who, acting under the delusion so prevalent in all manufacturing districts, have been guilty of very serious riots and acts of disturbance at Wotton-under-Edge and its neighbourhood some weeks ago. They proceeded to great violence, assaulting the operatives who undertook work at a lower rate than was approved by them, proceeding to the demolition of workshops and factories, meeting in large companies and debating in their clubs measures to obtain higher wages and control over their masters. Of these misguided men several were of very decent appearance; one had been a serjeant and enjoyed a pension. They must be punished with severity since the indulgence shown to the Stroud rioters has failed in its effect. The worst cases now will receive two years incarceration in one of the Houses of Correction.

January 21st, 1826

I returned home to serve my churches. I rode by way of Crickley Hill. Near Cubberley I noticed the new parsonage house which Mr. Hicks the incumbent is building there. A little beyond near the Severn Wells as they are called and which are assigned by some as the sources of the river Thames, a new turnpike road from Cirencester to Cheltenham is in progress. It will shorten and improve the communications between these towns. The ancient road ran nearly in the same direction.

January 27th, 1826

I left my family at Wellington Parade this afternoon being engaged to dine at my friend Mr. Howell's of Prinknash Park, whither I went in a post chaise. We had a large and very agreeably diversified party, the spirit of our host, his natural humour and extensive range of anecdote elicited from his guests correspondent sparks of intellectual power and varied commentary on men, matters, publications and opinions. Two young ladies as well as our hostess executed their musical talent in our favour. Mr. Macleod,

Mrs. Howell's brother, a barrister owing to his indifferent health, and the elegant Mrs. Frazer his sister, wife of a Captain in the Navy now on service in the West Indies, reside in a cottage of Howell's not far from Prinknash Park and were of the party. Mr. and Mrs. Wintle, and a lady with them. Mr. W. is a very worthy, good sort of man, residing at Saintbridge near Gloucester, and enjoying a handsome independence.

I slept at Prinknash Park in a curious old room where I was puzzled to explain an allegorical carving in wainscot, over the fireplace, which, indeed, I understand, as well as a device in the ceiling of the hall,[1] noticed by Lord Walpole[2] of antiquarian fame, is a mystery even to the cognoscenti. The device in the hall may probably be referred to the monastic times when the Abbots of Gloucester possessed Prinknash as a country residence. My chimney piece is of a later date and no doubt part of the decorations of some lay possessor of the latter half of the 17th or beginning of the 18th Century. The figures in relief, within a circular frame are three. One the one side a warrior, with helmet and sword, his shield laying at his feet, on the opposite side Justice with her sword and scales. The left arm of the warrior and the right arm of Justice equally elevated support a terrestrial globe, beneath which and between the two figures is in a smaller scale a youthful form, whether angel, female or juvenal I do not know, and he holds expanded, as if he were airing it at the fire, a garment; a very shirt or shift; and what it all means for my life I cannot conjecture.[3]

Saturday January 28th, 1826

My servant brought my horse from Gloucester and soon after breakfast I left my hospitable and agreeable friends for Upper Slaughter. Ascending from Prinknash I soon crossed the road from

1 A boss on the nave roof of the chapel, taken from the hall, has the combined emblems of York and Lancaster which may commemorate the recorded visit of Elizabeth of York, wife of Henry VII, in 1502.
2 Horace Walpole visited Prinknash and said: 'It stands on a glorious but impracticable hill, in the midst of a little forest of beech, and commanding Elyseum'.
3 In 1928 Thomas Dyer-Edwardes intended to leave Prinknash to the Benedictines of Caldy Island; but death intervened, and his grandson the Earl of Rothes carried out his wishes. However the house suffered some losses in the disappearance of two splendid seventeenth century chimney pieces, and the Jacobean furnishings of a complete room were sent to a museum in St. Louis, U.S.A.

Cheltenham to Painswick and took the direction of the old road between these places through Birdlip, which leads the traveller by a winding route, through the fine beech woods, which clothe the sides and summits of the hills in this part of the county. The day was fine and clear, and this part of my ride was almost novel to me, at least some years have elapsed since I had traversed it and in that time a very picturesque group of cottages has been erected in one of the glades, close by the road, to which the visitants of Cheltenham, who like Dr. Syntax,[1] make tours in search of the picturesque, fail not to resort. They are called Cranham Cottages and consist of several very tasteful thatched buildings with verandahs, painted casements, flower beds etc; looking exactly like one of those scenes which the theatre exhibits of rural elegance; or a description in a novel or a plan and view in Repton[2] or some other artist's elegant work on building cottages and laying out grounds.

A Mr. Todd has built them and resides there, not altogether as the elegant hermit of the beech woods, for he has a large interest and speculation in the beech timber growing around him, and on one occasion when he mingled in the society of Gloucester at a ball, wine had so drawn forth his vulgarity, that he insulted the company, was turned out of the room and forced to make a humble apology in the newspaper. But his cottages are not unworthy of a visit. From Birdlip I went to the top of Crickley Hill and so by the usual road home.

Monday January 30th, 1826
I returned to Gloucester, riding to Northleach, and proceeding from thence by the *Regulator*.

February 2nd, 1826
On my arrival at Cheltenham I found that my aunt, my mother's sister, had breathed her last about one o'clock this morning. She had a large acquaintance, had visited much in the middle part of life, had read and conversed and remembered much and retained her faculties to the last so that in many respects was a remarkable old person. Cheltenham had been her place of abode for many

---

1 William Combe (1741-1823) author of 'Dr. Syntax'.
2 Humphry Repton (1752-1818). Landscape-gardener.

Todd's Cottages at Cranham

Pearson Thompson

years. She was the eldest of four daughters of John Travell of Swerford, and on his demise they removed to Cheltenham as an eligible residence for single gentle-women, near their relatives at Stanway and Sandywell Park; a little country town, not then a public place. My mother was the youngest. For many years the unmarried sisters inhabited a house in the George Inn Yard, in former days one of the best houses in the place. It was there that I was born;[1] my mother, after several miscarriages, having come to Cheltenham to lie in, to avail herself of the skill of a celebrated accoucheur of the place, the late Mr. Clark.

February 8th, 1826
......walked up the Sherborne Well walk and as far as Thompson's Montpellier Pump Room. The proprietor Mr. Pearson Thompson is building there on a very large scale. He is greatly extending the pump room and its contiguous buildings and will doubtless make it, by next summer, a very sumptuous edifice. Reading, billiard and promenade rooms are to be under the same roof, and the whole to be surmounted by a dome covered with copper, in the elevation of which many workmen are now employed. Others at work planting ornamental shrubberies, etc. in the field in front of the Pump room and public walks.[2]

April 1st, 1826
The building project on the other side of the town, on Mr. Pitt's estate is however in abeyance, the pecuniary embarrassments of the bankers probably account for this.[3]

1 26 February, 1783
2 In 1824 Pearson Thompson asked John (Buonarotti) Papworth to prepare a scheme for the Lansdown estate, so Papworth planned the first English garden city with houses set among formal avenues and gardens. Part of the scheme had to be abandoned in 1825, owing to a local financial crisis caused by land speculation at Pittville. Papworth's Montpellier Pump Room is a masterpiece with a domed roof lit after the manner of the Pantheon.
3 The unfortunate architect William Jay, who had a successful career in Savannah, returned to England in 1824. In Cheltenham he designed Columbia Place in 1825-1826. In the Museum there is a drawing for Pittville Parade by William Jay 1826. This terrace survives in Evesham road. He also designed houses in Priory Street before he went bankrupt in 1829, as well as Watermoor House, Cirencester, for Pitt's solicitor, Mullings.

The Bagmen's Banquet at the Bell Inn, Cheltenham.

Engraved by Robt. Cruikshank.

Published by Sherwood & Co.

May 10th, 1826

Attended the primary visitation of the Archdeacon of Gloucester, Dr. Timbrill, at Stow.[1] He preached a good moderate sermon on the duties of the Christian ministry, which would have been more useful had it been less general. His vehement and authoritative manner on one or two occasions both to the Churchwardens, and to the Clergy, to the latter on the subject of apologies for not attending being omitted by some absent incumbents and curates, excited a little prejudice against him; his principle was right, his manner of explaining it wrong. Fourteen of the clergy dined with him, and everything went off pleasantly. There was no charge: it is not customary in this diocese.[2]

June 30th, 1826

At Stanway. Lady Elcho had invited Sir Thomas Phillipps to dinner. He came from Middle Hill alone, his buxom and forward lady being at Cheltenham. He was in good spirits, though he has just lost a contested Election, having been induced to offer himself for the borough of Grimsby, with little prospect of success. This was unlucky as he can ill afford to throw away money.[3]

July 1st, 1826

We returned home (from Stanway) arriving about 3 o'clock. The weather was intensely hot, as indeed it has been for some time past. The long continued drought is remarkable; the hay made during

---

1 Although they cannot usually afford to live in their historic rectories and vicarages and have to squeeze into little concrete boxes, I was pleased with the timeless titles of the clergy when I attended the Archdeacon's (Evans) visitation at Stow in 1976: the Rector of Stow-on-the- Wold; the Rector of Batsford with Moreton-in-Marsh; the vicar of Bledington; the Rector of Bourton-on-the-Hill; the Officiating Chaplain to Her Majesty's Forces; the Rector of Bourton-on-the-Water; the Priest in charge of Great Rissington and Rural Dean of Gloucester Cathedral; the Rector of Broadwell with Evenlode, the Vicar of the Guitings, with Cutsdean, and Farmcote; the Rector of Longborough with Condicote and Sezincote; the Canon of Marshonaland; the Rector of Oddington and Adlestrop; the Rector of little Rissington and Honorary Canon of Gloucester Cathedral; the Rector of Upper and Lower Slaughter with Eyford and Naunton; the Vicar of Upper and Nether Swell; the Rector of Todenham with Lower Lemington; the Rector of Westcote with Icomb.

2 Means Archdeacon's charge (instructions) not "paying for his dinner".

3 Witts was in a position to know this as he was owed £6,000 on mortgage by Phillipps.

this dry season is excellent in quality but very deficient in quantity; the springs are exceedingly low, the wheat looks promising but the barley and oats thirst for rain; the pastures are sadly burnt, and the promise of turnips is very small.

July 10th, 1826

I left home for Gloucester to attend the Quarter Sessions, riding to Cheltenham. While I was waiting for the coach at Cheltenham I walked to Sherborne Spa,[1] near which the proprietors have erected a building to contain a very elegant work of art, a marble basin with statuary and figures remarkably well sculptured. It is the work of a foreign artist, and estimated at a high price. The mineral water is made to pass into the vase through the mouth of one of the animals or birds. It appeared disfigured by the meanness of the building in which it was placed, where Doric fluted columns in front strangely contrast with a naked wall behind the urn perforated at one side by a vulgar square window, and a door in the corner leading to the penthouse, where the attendant waits the arrival of the bilious votaries of the nymph of the Spring and Urn.

A new street at right angles with the High Street on the northern side is in progress, which will connect the High Street with Portland Street.

July 14th, 1826

I had intended to return home this evening but had since I came to Gloucester received a letter intimating on the part of Lady Elcho that I should come to Stanway before Lord Wemyss left on Monday. At Cheltenham I therefore took a post chaise for Stanway. It is some time since I travelled this road. On leaving the town I observed a little progress made towards the great projected enlargement of the place in the new town proposed to be erected on Mr. Pitt's estate: probably the late convulsions and particularly the stoppage of Turner's and Hartland's banks have arrested the building mania: only a few handsome shells of houses and a very noble-looking pumproom are in course of erection. The road through Prestbury and Southam continues very narrow and bad.

Lord Wemyss's removal to and from his seat in Scotland is always contrived to be by sea, while part of his family travel by

1 The Queen's Hotel was later built on the site of the Sherborne Spa.

land. Nothing could be more pleasing and cheerful than his lordship's manner among his friends and relatives at Stanway. Lady Wemyss, now on a very large scale, retains many of those attractions which have made her so popular ... A noisy but not unskilled band of music from Broadway played most of the evening in the hall, and a promiscuous dance among the gentry and domestics was kicked up.

August 5th, 1826 Gloucester

In the course of the day I met my acquaintance Mr. Charles Cripps, who resides here as manager of the Branch establishment of the Bank of England, which has recently commenced its operations at Gloucester. This is the only branch which the great bank has yet thrown out, and will serve as a model for others. Cripps is well calculated to superintend its operations, having long been the active partner with his father and uncle at Cirencester and Stow as country bankers, from which partnership, of-course, he has withdrawn on undertaking the management of the Gloucester Branch Bank. At present it will disappoint the neighbourhood, as the latitude afforded by country bankers will not be given; no customer will be allowed to overdraw his account, no advances will be made on doubtful pledges etc.

August 6th, 1826

Messrs. Hurd and Winter having kindly engaged to do my duty at Upper Slaughter and Lower Swell I was enabled to pass this day without hurrying home to return again to the trial to-morrow. I attended Divine Service in the forenoon at the Cathedral, which was extremely crowded. The Judges with their suite, the Sheriff, Mr. Hale, many of the county magistrates, a large proportion of the gentlemen of the bar, etc. were present. It was altogether a very imposing sight, and the Bishop preached an excellent sermon on the Day of Judgement. After service I was obliged to go to Mr. Mutlow's[1] (the organist) to hold a consultation on matters relative

1 The 19th Century organists at Gloucester Cathedral were
William Mutlow 1782-1832
John Arnott 1832-1865
S.S. Wesley 1865-1876
Charles Harford Lloyd 1876-1882
C. Lee Williams 1882-1897
A. Herbert Brewer 1897-1928

to the approaching Music meeting. I met there Mr. Cramer the celebrated violinist and leader of the orchestra who had come from Cheltenham. He assisted us with his valuable counsel; I found him a very well-bred, sensible and intelligent man.

Being strongly pressed by my friend Howell who had sent a horse for me in the morning, I rode out to dinner at Prinknash Park.

August 7th, 1826

Before 9 o'clock I was on the alert to attend the hearing of the much canvassed Sandywell cause.[1] Vehicles of all sorts from Cheltenham had been pouring in with the curious, all on the tiptoe of expectation and large importations of witnesses had arrived on both sides. The doors of the Shire Hall were besieged by a dense mob, chiefly of well-dressed persons, and lawyer's wigs curiously mingled in the throng of white beaver hats and Leghorn bonnets. I called as I went down Westgate Street on Mr. Newmarch who conducts the case for the prosecution and found him in great dismay because no leader had appeared for the plaintiffs and they could not go to trial without one.

August 31st, 1826

Walked with my cousins the Misses Witts to their pretty village of Hempsted. They occupy for the summer apartments in a cottage close to the grounds of the mansion house, which is the seat of the Lysons family. The Rev. Daniel Lysons,[2] the antiquary, is the present proprietor, having succeeded to it on the death of his brother,[3] the still more distinguished antiquary. The brothers united in the publication of several important and interesting antiquarian and topographical works. Mr. D. Lysons, Rector of Rodmarton, an elderly man is now abroad with his family. Lord John Somerset, younger brother of the Duke of Beaufort occupies the seat. He is in the Army. The parsonage is a very pretty spot and a good old house near the church. A Mr. Jones, son to an Alderman and Brushmaker of Gloucester, is the new incumbent,

---

1 A matter of a disputed will and the inheritance of Sandywell Park.
2 Daniel Lysons, (1762-1834). Topographer.
3 Samuel Lysons, (1763-1819). Antiquary. Author of 'A Collection of Gloucestershire Antiquities', 1804, and discoverer of the Woodchester Roman pavement in 1793.

having bought the next presentation of the heirs of the late Duchess of Norfolk.

September 1st, 1826

We made a very pleasant excursion to-day and were not home till late in the evening. We went in and outside of Mrs. Hunt's chariot. Berkeley Castle, and the great works now in progress for the completion of the Berkeley and Gloucester canal at Sharpness Point, were the objects in view.

To Berkeley the distance is 16 miles. We were not long in reaching Quedgley Green, whence I had a distant view of Elmore Court, the place where I first went to school. It is a deserted mansion of Sir. W. Guise's. In 1793 when I was an inmate a highly respectable academy was kept there by two clergymen, brothers-in-law; some of my old school-fellows are among my intimate acquaintance in the county and sitting on the same bench with me as magistrates, General Guise, Col. Webb, M.P. for Gloucester etc.: others, as the Raikeses are now removed from the county. Beyond, where the road to Stroud and Rodborough diverges to the left through a fine country, the clothing valleys of Gloucestershire, we passed Hardwicke Court the mansion of my friend T.J. Lloyd Baker, lately High Sheriff of the county. The principal attractions to the traveller on this road are the eminences confining the great vale of Severn, fine bold heights with masses of beech woods; some of the hills project like bastions into the plain. In the winding valleys among them are the picturesque dells of Chalford, Woodchester, etc. so well-known for their busy crowded population of manufacturers in the different departments of the clothing trade. Machinery and millworks bestride the once limpid brooks long dyed a deep blue by the processes carried on. The views from the summits of all these hills, particularly Robins Wood, Painswick, Standish Park, Frocester, Uley Bury, and Stinchcombe, are superb. At Whitminster is the seat of Mr. Cambridge, who resides wholly in Gloucestershire. We often meet as Governors of the Infirmary, and he is a singular character but estimable. Cambridge Inn, or rather Inns, for there are more than one, is a resting place between Gloucester and Newport and forms a hamlet not far from Slimbridge, a village with an elegant steeple to the right of the road. We passed the Stroud-water canal, the length of this is rather more than 8 miles from Stroud to Framilode where it enters the Severn.

Diverging from the Bristol road we soon arrived at Berkeley

Berkeley Castle

situated in a fertile valley embowered in trees. The unusual verdure after such a season of drought fully proved the richness of the soil and luxuriance of the vegetation. The castle is hidden by a belt of trees; the deer park is at a distance, nor is much of the modern taste of gardening visible. The town itself is mean; a new and handsome market house and town hall has recently been erected. We found a very comfortable inn, and baited the horses, while we went to survey the castle. This we hastened to do in the absence of the owner, Colonel Berkeley, whom we had met before we entered the town on horseback escorting two equestrian females of doubtful character.

Pity it is that this fine handsome, talented man who had capacity and powers of mind and wealth at his command, amply sufficient to redeem the cloud under which he was born, whose very disadvantages entailed on him by the errors of his parents, would have pleaded in his favour with the liberal, should have thrown away the promising game which he held in his hand and debased himself so far as to become the slave of stormy passions, the seducer, the profligate swearer, the amateur actor, the corrupter of youth, the victim of violence of temper, the King of a company of *roués.*

Between the inn and the castle is the home of the late Dr. Jenner, the benefactor of mankind, who began and closed his career in this place. It is now the occasional residence of his son, a dissipated man, who has felt all the baneful influence of the contiguity to the Castle and its unprincipled owner.

The church is large and is believed to have been built in the reign of Henry II. The tower is comparatively modern. Below the churchyard, and on the brow of the rocky hill, overlooking rich and extensive meadows, is the castle which as a habitable mansion preserves its original character more than any similar structure in the Kingdom.

To enter into the disgraceful story of the late Earl and his Countess, the parents of the present illegitimate owner, would be too tedious here. [1] A younger brother of the Colonel is the actual

1 The fifth Earl of Berkeley and Mary Cole had thirteen children, of which the first seven were deemed to be illegitimate. The eldest son William (1786-1857) was called Lord Dursley until his father's death in 1810. This was the courtesy title of the eldest son of the family. He then began calling himself Earl of Berkeley until the 1811 decision of the House of Lords declared him illegitimate. Thereafter he became known as Colonel Berkeley. In 1831, however, he was created Lord Segrave, and in 1841 Earl Fitzhardinge. This explains why he appears in Francis Witts' diary under

peer, being the eldest son after the real marriage of his parents; but he is never seen in the county, and it is said, rejects the title considering his elder brothers legitimate, whom the House of Lords decided to be otherwise. Much mystery still hangs about the family arrangements. Lady Berkeley lives at Cranford in Middlesex.

At the castle gate in sullen indolence crouched a huge old mastiff, a breed of dog, which is a great favourite with the present owner. The stranger is required to insert his name and residence in a book kept for the purpose, and the housekeeper appears to conduct you round the castle. As the Colonel was now out riding we were easily admitted into his private appartments, a breakfast room and music or drawing room fitted up by Lady Berkeley. The breakfast room is full of pictures indicative of Col. Berkeley's tastes. One represents a group of portraits of hounds and hunters, another a bloody affray by night in a thicket between a party of desperate poachers and determined keepers. The adventure occurred in 1816, and a life was lost. I noticed also a miniature of Dr.Jenner,an excellent likeness.From this room we were conducted thro' a series of steep passages, narrow, dark, and intricate, up and down stairs, in and out of antiquated bedrooms, full of antiquated tapestry, carved and worm-eaten bedsteads, some elevated in recesses higher than the rest of the floor, some in which prince or queen or potentate had slept, most with concealed doors but all in use when the castle is full of company. There is a curious cabin bed or cot, chiefly of ebony, which was part of the furniture of Sir

so many different names.

The cause of the trouble was the fact that Mary Cole was born the daughter of a Gloucester butcher. However, she thought at first that she was properly married to Lord Berkeley on March 30th, 1785, at Berkeley church. This marriage was subsequently not considered legal as indeed it presumably was not, and Lord and Lady Berkeley went through a second marriage ceremony in 1796. Only the children born after the second marriage were considered to be legitimate by the House of Lords and so the sixth son Moreton became the next Earl of Berkeley. He was the mildest of Mary Cole's sons, the rest were all violent men. He never claimed the property, and Berkeley Castle remained the possession of Earl Fitzhardinge, till his death in 1857, when his next illegitimate brother succeeded to the Castle and was created Baron Fitzhardinge. This Lord Fitzhardinge had two sons, who in due course succeeded him: both died without children, the second in 1916.

These later Fitzhardinges were excellent landowners and much respected in Gloucestershire. "Their rule at Berkeley" says Hope Costley-White, "like that of Mary, their grandmother, was beneficent and wise."

Craven Berkeley, who was legitimate, only left a daughter, therefore the Earldom passed on Moreton's death to a cousin, whose son became the last Earl of Berkeley, and the title is now extinct. However, the castle is still owned and occupied by the Berkeley family.

Francis Drake's vessel when he circumnavigated the world, but too crazy to admit of the weight of a degenerate modern, so it is never used. There is a tradition that there were two dungeons in the castle, one is said to be filled up. Out of the other the late Countess, for so she may be styled, though yet living, as she does not and ought not to mix in society with the noble and the good, caused the rubbish to be removed, and there it is in a gloomy room without light. The housekeeper lifts a trapdoor and lowers a lanthorn with a lighted candle, and this is the dungeon. We visited the castle leads. The stables at a little distance look like a modern Gothic mansion. Close beneath the castle terrace are the pheasant nurseries, vast numbers of young birds are brought up here under the protection of the keepers, fed from the terrace by the Colonel and his guests and finally turned out to add to the winged multitude, which swarm over the manor in all directions. Returning to the interior of the castle, the little chamber said to be the scene of the second Edward's barbarous murder was the next sight.

In a picture of the death of Julius Caesar, Brutus with the reeking dagger is a portrait of Col. Berkeley, and records the Colonel's partiality to the *métier* of an actor which he delights to exercise to admiring and good natured audiences in Cheltenham, Gloucester and Tewkesbury.

The tour of the castle was made ... and we proceeded to Sharpness Point. Large herds of cows grazing in spacious pastures remind one of the cheese for which the Hundred of Berkeley is so famous. The taste and ruling passion of the Berkeley family were here developed in the abundance of pheasants, feeding in the fields and on the edges of little thickets and coverts, they were so many as to give the idea of domestic fowls. The farm which we were crossing and also Sharpness Point has been left to Lady Berkeley and is at present hers. She has shown good taste in her admiration of the spot and her desire to adorn it and erected a commodious cottage now occupied by an intelligent gamekeeper and fisherman, which she had surrounded with a garden and plantation, now of more than 20 years growth, through which walks lead to the turf carpeted promontory properly called Sharpness Point. This is studded by a few dwarf oaks, overhanging the rocks, which form the basis of the promontory; a seat is placed here and there but all prettiness has been avoided, and it really is an enjoyable spot, commanding fine views when the tide is up, and where a company of friends might most discuss a picnic dinner, and ruralize, and forget for a season the vexations and serious cares of life.

The Severn is here ¾ mile across. The opposite shore which is moderately elevated is in the parish of Lydney. The tide was out and in the channel were fishermen wading up to their middle driving hand nets before them, trying to catch shrimps. The contrivances for catching salmon in wicker baskets suspended in wooden frames in straight lines towards the current, were beneath our feet.

At the foot of Sharpness Point are the great works in progress for completing the Gloucester Berkeley Canal, a speculation which has been lingering for many years, but seems at last proceeding towards the realization of the schemes of the projectors. The work was begun in 1794 and the object was to avoid the tortuous and dangerous navigation of the Severn to Gloucester, which indeed was only practicable at high tides. The project has at various times been quite at a stop. Of late years the energies of the subscribers have revived and a great effort has been made and Mr. Telford the engineer put in authority, to superintend the completion of the work. The canal has in great measure been excavated throughout the whole line, bridges erected, and the docks and basin near the quay at Gloucester in a great state of forwardness. The Proprietors are now building at Gloucester a range of Warehouses suitable to the expected trade.

Telford first came up (from Eskdale) as a mason to London about 1782 to work at the Adelphi, then building. His talent and scientific turn of mind, with the patronage of powerful and discerning men, among whom was Sir James Pulteney, who employed him largely on his estates and collieries, canals, etc. in Shropshire, have greatly advanced him to the very summit of his profession.

September 5th, 1826

The Stratford and Moreton railway was opened this day for the conveyance of goods from the former to the latter place, and a vast concourse of persons assembled at Moreton-in-Marsh. The market of this town, disused for a very long period, has on this occasion been revived with great spirit and will in some respects be injurious to the market at Stow-on-the-Wold. At an early hour in the evening all the provisions of the town were exhausted, the roasted ox demolished and neither bread nor beer to be had for love or money. The committee preceded the coal waggons with a band of music, and all was joyous. Behind the scenes, however, the proprietors have reason to mourn over mismanagement, exhausted means, and scant hopes even of distant remuneration; but the public will no doubt be considerable gainers.

September 11th, 1826

I left home at an early hour for Gloucester on horse-back and proceeding by Crickley Hill, arrived at Wellington Parade soon after 11 o'clock, finding my dear wife and her mother pretty well. The music meeting being now close at hand I was engaged in some of the preliminary arrangements.

September 13th, 1826

The town was all alive with company, some crowding towards the college, some arriving at the inns and lodgings, all in gay attire and nothing could be more lovely than the weather. A large posse of constables under the able generalship of a Bow Street Officer was posted at the Cathedral door, and their services were likely to be needed for the admission this morning was free. Each Steward's share of tickets for the galleries was 25, and the lay and clerical galleries held about 60 persons and were each day almost exclusively occupied by the first ladies in point of rank and connection, who attended the meeting, a most beautiful sight and the present style of female dress tended to justify the appellations affixed, a parterre — a bed of roses. My own ladies were each day accommodated in the first row of the clerical gallery, and from the extent of my acquaintance I was each morning soon drained of my tickets, and had I twice as many could have disposed of them to various applicants. By 11 o'clock the inner choir of the Cathedral was fearfully crowded ... an occasional scream or groan indicated distress or fainting, some were carried out, some struggled into the outer choir, the most persevering stood their ground. The whole was opened with Handel's sublime Overture to Esther....

The concert at the Shire Hall was very fully attended, nearly a thousand persons were present and the pressure at the upper end of the room very great. Lady Lyttelton and the Misses Witts were there and as soon as I had provided for their accommodation by a fresh bench between those already occupied and the orchestra, the well-known and obtrusive Alderman Matthew Wood[1] of London, coveting similar accommodation addressed himself to me. I explained it had been the constant rule with the Stewards to reserve

---

1 Two silver cups presented in 1820 and 1821 to Sir Matthew Wood M.P. Lord Mayor of London, for the part he played in championing the cause of Queen Caroline, are now in possession of the City of Gloucester.

accommodation for their own parties, and with very few forms kept back and the Lord Lieutenant not yet arrived he would have to find accommodation in the seats already placed. In reply the Alderman (who since the death of the sister of his namesake the eccentric and wealthy Jemmy Wood, Banker of Gloucester, has been a summer resident here where the old lady left him a good house in consideration of his championship of the late Queen Caroline, and where he hopes to worm himself into the good graces of Banker Jemmy,) dilated on the ill-usage of the public by the stewards: then exit in a rage. When the conversation reached the ears of Bowles[1] the following day when we were summing up the receipts at the Cathedral door, the poet extemporised:—

> What money our music produces;
> For surely a meeting is good
> Where are Beauforts and Sherbornes and Ducies
> And Lansdownes and Alderman Wood.

The receipts for the charity amounted to £816.1.8d.

At the close of the concert I remained an hour assisting in the *devoirs* of the tea rooms, and enjoying while I strolled about with my friend Howell, the profusions of the youthful in merry dance; here a high-born fastidious group in graceful meanders moving in the light quadrille, there a less well-bred but equally well-satisfied dandy, perchance an attorney's clerk, balancing and pointing a fantastic toe, opposite to some rosy good humoured country girl, a belle from Stroud or Tewkesbury.

September 16th, 1826

I was required to be on the wing again, and after luncheon mounted my pony, which I had brought with me on Monday, and riding home by Crickley Hill reached Upper Slaughter before tea time.

The total amount of the expenses (for this music meeting) was £2,702.6.8d: the receipts for tickets sold and books of the performance, £2,393.12.6d, and each steward had a surplus to pay of £51.9.0d. This is a heavy and grievous tax on individuals, particularly on clergymen standing forward to promote a charitable and social meeting.[2]

---

1 Rev. W.L. Bowles, another steward.
2 Witts was thanked for "he deserved all the credit for the arrangement of the music, and the details of the festival".

September 26th, 1826

Margaret and myself dined at Prinknash Park. The Howells are soon to return to Gibraltar where he after more than a year's leave of absence is about to resume the duties of Judge Advocate and Civil Judge. Mr. and Mrs. Hyett from Painswick dined.

September 27th, 1826

After breakfast at Prinknash Park we took a walk on the terrace and in the grounds, admiring the magnificent view which this hill affords. The horses came to take us back to Gloucester but we did not proceed to the race course, which was a great object of attraction. These races are revived, after being discontinued; but are not generally approved. The stewards are Colonel Berkeley, and Mr. R. Canning, who presided at a Ball given at the Bell Inn this evening.

September 29th, 1826

They say the march of intellect is wonderful these days. Men navigate by steam, tram carts travel by steam; but this is nothing to the present fashion of travelling by paper kites. To-day we witnessed the experiment made at Gloucester. For some days I had noticed two large paper kites hovering over the town. They were hoisted by a school master who amused himself with mechanical pursuits, letting off balloons etc. The wind being westerly, was favourable for an excursion to Cheltenham so he orders out his gig, or rather I think it was a four wheeled chair, attaches it to two paper kites, mounts with two or three companies and away they go, not very rapidly, not at a very regular pace, but progressing. The corners are turned cleverly by the charioteer sitting on a kind of dickey, beneath which the string of his kites is wound round a cylinder acted on by a winch. As for the kites they are careering steadily, one considerably in advance of the other, and at a much greater height. The cord attached to the further passes through the centre of the nearer, so one cord is attached to both, and both work in the same direction, thus double power is gained. The drive to Cheltenham was no doubt safely accomplished as we set out soon after and did not overtake them.

We stopped at Cheltenham for half an hour and walked to the Montpellier Spa to view a very magnificent room which Mr. Pearson Thompson has erected. We found it a very fine edifice surmounted by a dome covered in copper. The space beneath is circular and fitted up with great taste and simplicity.[1] There are, I believe, four fireplaces and above them mirrors. It is used as a promenade, and fashion now consecrates it as her throne to the depreciation of the assembly rooms, the balls there being eclipsed by the quadrilles here, at which visitors are not expected to appear in ball dresses ... and speculating matrons, chaperoning fair and elegant but slenderly endowed nymphs with taper waists, and elderly bachelors from the banks of the Ganges with injured livers and bilious complexions, smile their approbation.

A handsome street, leading at right angles from the High Street towards Portland Street, parallel to Winchcombe Street, is in considerable forwardness, a good substitute for a narrow alley for foot passengers formerly leading in the same direction.

We did not reach home till the evening had closed in.

October 7th, 1826

I rode to Chipping Norton to prepare for a design to erect a tablet, recording the deaths of my revered parents in the church. Before I reached the town I met the incumbent, Mr. Skillern, who was master of the Crypt School in Gloucester and whose benefice is in the gift of the Dean and Chapter. Since I last visited the place for my mother's funeral, the tower of the church has been rebuilt. It was taken down being considered insecure. The new tower is well proportioned and in good taste, built of freestone; the only fault that struck me was the pinnacles being rather too low. The centre aisle is very lofty and lighted by large windows over the arches in what, I believe, is called the clerestory.

In the pillar which supported the rood loft on the north, is worked a flight of stone steps the summit of which is level with the top of the present screen. In the same relative situation we found a flight of steps when the enlargement of Upper Slaughter church took place some years ago. No doubt a part of the service was performed by the Roman Catholic ecclesiastics in the rood loft. Here probably the deacon read the gospel, attended by the sub-deacon holding the book and two clerks bearing candles. On the back of the pillar containing the staircase I intend to place the tablet to the memory of my parents and brother.

1 By J.B. Papworth, but Witts does not mention this.

December 30th, 1826

I rode to Chipping Norton and back to see the monument now erected by me to the memory of my dear parents and brother and was well satisfied with it.

April 2nd, 1827

We walked to Over Bridge to view the site of the new bridge over the Severn, building under the direction of Mr. Telford, by the County. The work is in progress; many labourers, excavators, etc. were employed. On one side the masonry of an abutment is in a forward state, on the other they are driving the piles. There were collected great heaps of fine stone ready squared in large blocks, of different sorts, for the foundation and superstructure. A steam engine was erecting, and several cranes were in operation, lifting masses of stone from the barges in which they were conveyed.

Good Friday, April 13th, 1827

Attended at the Cathedral which was extremely crowded, and, although early there, could not get a sitting in the inner choir. The vergers arranged the matter ill, introducing many into the stalls, who had no other titles than a silver key, and excluding others, members of the grand jury and magistrates, on the plea, that the judges and their train would require all the reserved seats. The excluded members, to the number of 15 or 20, then resorted to one of the galleries; but that was locked, and the Jack in office there refused to open the door, because the seats were appropriated to the College school boys, and they must be accommodated first. Thus baffled we had no other remedy than forcible entry, and clambering, with what agility we could, over the door, we were soon seated. However, the crowd below was so dense, the chanter and reader underneath us were so muttering and monotonous, the altar and pulpit so distant, and so much of solid masonry interposed that I, at least, heard next to nothing of the service.

April 19th, 1827

I attended the Crown Court, and heard a very interesting trial for maliciously shooting with intent to murder. The two prisoners, brothers of the name of Dyer, had been charged by an accomplice, Thomas Mills, with burglary, and at the last Assizes were acquitted. All belonged to what has received the appellation of the Wickwar gang.

Malice is then presumed to have actuated the Dyers. A shot was fired into a cottage, in which Mills with his wife and family were sitting round a bright fire. The contents of the gun, evidently directed at Mills, came in contact with the back of a chair and lodged in the left side of his wife, who providentially survived the shot. Evidence was given that the Dyers had spoken in a threatening manner, as if determined to be revenged on Mills. The brothers set up an alibi, and much minuteness of detail as to time and place was sworn by their witnesses. The jury divested themselves of any hesitation, which the confident assertions of the witnesses for the alibi might have given rise to; indeed the discrepancy of country clocks was taken into consideration. The issue was a verdit of guilty with a recommendation for mercy; but the learned Judge gave little hopes of their lives being saved; and left them for execution.

April 26th, 1827

This day was a great holiday in Gloucester. The Berkeley canal, now fully completed, being opened. Two large vessels, with a considerable number of smaller ones, arrived in the afternoon in the canal basin, amid the greetings of many thousand spectators, having performed successfully the voyage from the basin at Sharpness Point. One of these ships was a three-master, a large square-rigged vessel, the other a brig. In the evening I saw them moored in the spacious basin, bedecked with flags and streamers, and surrounded by a gaping crowd; tents and booths with liquor and refreshments lined the margin of the basin. The Canal Company has erected a very large range of warehouses contiguous, and provided that no impediment interferes from shifting sands in the Severn at the mouth of the canal, the great work now accomplished will be of infinite service to the city and this part of the country.[1]

1 The Gloucestershire Society for Industrial Archaeology, observed the one hundred and fiftieth anniversary in 1977. Francis Witts was quite right. The opening of the canal made a vast difference to the economic importance of the city.

April 28th, 1827

As we went towards Cheltenham, we marvelled at the crowds of people of the lower orders trudging on towards Gloucester, with great eagerness, young and middle aged and many females. We knew not of any Fair or race or merry meeting: at last the truth flashed on my recollection, all these people were hurrying to witness the execution of the wretched brothers Dyer who are to expiate their crimes this morning by their deaths.

April 28th, 1827

We remained an hour or more in Cheltenham and strolled towards Pittville so far as to have a distant view of the new Pumproom, a stately edifice after the Grecian model; some rows of houses, of large dimensions, and one or two tasteful villas of moderate size are in progress of erection in the grounds, and this will be an elegant quarter of this luxurious and straggling resort of fashion.

June 30th, 1827

The weather being fine, we took a drive to call on Lady Elcho at Stanway, who has been arrived from London some days, but unfortunately her Ladyship was gone to Cheltenham. On our return in the afternoon we called for half an hour at Mr. Bowen's parsonage at Temple Guiting, who shewed us his handsome church, and took us a little circuit in Mr. Talbot's grounds which are very pleasantly and tastefully laid out, the ground being undulating, the meadows rich and now all alive with haymakers, the distant plantations covering the horizon, the groves under which we strolled cool and umbrageous, the lawns pleasantly broken with single trees and bordered with thickets, the walks neatly kept, the grotto cool and dark, all bespeaking good taste and opulence. The family is in town: so it is that fashionable people desert their country seats, their rich parks and lovely gardens in the finest season and live there only in the gloomiest months of the year; for when the London season is over, fashion dictates a second edition on an inferior scale at some sea-bathing or watering place or some rambling tour in search of ever-eluding pleasure.

July 3rd, 1827

We took a drive to Adlestrop to pay the compliment of a

wedding visit to Mr. and Mrs. Twisleton, the young rector having lately married the Hon. Emily Wingfield. The lady possesses more blood than beauty; but is represented to be amiable and accomplished; these good qualities make up for a small fortune. Twisleton has lately published an octavo volume in divinity, a new edition of Archbishop Wake's Catechism in which he has interwoven the texts of scripture ... but I am inclined to think Love's Labour lost, for it was better as it was before.

July 6th, 1827

Attended the quarterly petty Sessions at Northleach Bridewell, at which being Visiting Magistrate I presided. Afterwards I dined at Mr. Waller's at Farmington, meeting Mr. and Mrs. Boudier and Mrs. Waller and her two daughters. Mr. Waller seems a very promising young man. I have known him from boyhood, though we never exchanged visits at Farmington during his father's life time, who was far from estimable, and whose latter years were spent in Boulogne where so many impoverished English gentry resort to. Farmington is suitable for field sports, and now that it is in good repair and well fitted up, it is a very comfortable residence. Waller has married a young lady whom he met at Boulogne, well connected, accomplished, pleasing, elegant and handsome but with little fortune. Mrs. Waller, senior, with her two daughters and a younger sons, two school boys, occupies Mr. Willan's mansion house in the village. Mr. Boudier, once Mr. Waller's private tutor, and to whom he gave the living of Farmington, occupies the parsonage, so that there are three cheerful, rational, friendly families grouped agreeably together. Mr. Waller himself, under an unpromising exterior, seems to possess good sense and principles, with the desire of making himself useful as a country gentleman; for the duties of the Magistracy he appears to have a turn, and most desirable it is that the younger squires should engage in the county business and not leave all to the clergy, as is too often the case, while their attention is absorbed in fox hunting, racing, London amusements, or the gay frivolities of Cheltenham, Brighton, etc.

September 3rd, 1827

We drove to make our first call on Mrs. Hastings at Daylesford. It has pleased this ancient lady (Warren Hasting's widow), after we had been 18 years settled here, to find us out and visit us: and though we did not particularly covet an introduction, yet we had no disinclination to accept the tardy civility. We found Mrs. H. and her German relative, Miss Chapuset, at home, and were very politely received. The mistress of the mansion is a very fine old lady, at a very advanced age; but full of spirit, talent and conversation, graceful and elegant. She must have been very attractive, beautiful and talented when she engrossed the affections of one of the ablest men of his age, as well as the most ill-treated, the quondam Governor General of India.

Mr. Hastings, returning to India, made the acquaintance on the voyage with his lady, then Baroness d'Imhoff, whose husband was proceeding to the East to follow the profession of a portrait painter. Mr. Hastings was captivated; Baron d'Imhoff was not particular and an arrangement was made. The portrait painting scheme thus interrupted, the Baron returned to Germany with a replenished purse and the Baroness married the Governor General. Mr. Hasting's public life, and his private life in latter years, are highly to be praised. The House and grounds at Daylesford were built and laid out by him. The structure is somewhat in Eastern taste and striking, the views extensive over Adlestrop, Oddington and towards Stow; the grounds are well planted, the flower gardens near the house, and there is a winding sheet of water at some distance in a valley. There are some good paintings; in the library a curious piece by Zoffany, a painter who went to India. It represents a cock-fight[1]. There are portraits of the Duke and Duchess of Gloucester, and a large landscape representing a scene in Mrs. Hasting's life. She had heard of her husband's illness in Calcutta, when at a considerable distance up the Ganges and was bent upon resorting to his bedside; but everything was forbidding, the appearance of the weather, the state of the river, all were unfavourable. The painter has embodied on his canvass the moment when the strange-looking Eastern barge, with its wild copper-coloured mariners directing it through the lashed waves and surf, is striving to gain the land. .

The day was fine, our drive agreeable and we returned home pleased.

---

1 Exhibited at the National Portrait Gallery, January 1977

September 21st, 1827

We were to have dined with Mrs. Hastings at Daylesford, but our horses disappointed us, not coming till an hour after the time fixed for our setting out. We were therefore obliged to send our servant on horse-back with our apology.

September 25th, 1827

Mrs. Hastings most politely invited us this day to make up for the disappointment, and we reached Daylesford by 6 o'clock. We were received in one of the drawing rooms through the library, remarkable for its suite of ivory chairs and sofas, curious articles of luxury but not to be used by the male creation. Mr. Winter officiated as chaplain and carved the haunch of venison. Mr. and Mrs. Twisleton from Adlestrop were accompanied by Mrs. T's mother the Lady Powerscourt and her sister Miss Wingfield. The sisters during the evening sang pleasingly together, without music or with the mere accompaniment of the guitar.

October 12th, 1827

I inspected the treadwheel at Northleach Bridewell, recently put up. The machinery still requires some alterations. The velocity with which the wheel revolved was too great so that the fatigue exceeded the strength of the prisoners. The revolutions should be limited to about 52 steps in a minute. A regulator must be applied to the machine in such a manner as to compensate for any difference in the weight of the gangs on the wheel, whether grown men or boys. The millwright was in attendance. It is intended to keep the machine going, should there at any time be a failure of corn to grind. Nine or ten prisoners were on the mill at once, they worked each 4½ or 5 minutes, one descending from the extremity of the wheel every half minute. A relay of prisoners is kept in an adjacent yard, walking in a circle.

December 6th, 1827

We called at Wormington Grange. Mr. Gist is making large additions to the house, and employs Mr. Hakewell as an architect, an artist of considerable reputation in his line: the place proposed seems very suitable and the structure will be simple and gentlemanlike, while the interior will be very commodious.

July 15th, 1828 Gloucester

Walked to view the new Over Bridge. The arch is now completed and the centres removed. It is indeed the most beautiful structure; the span of the arch exceeds any other in the Kingdom, and it is peculiar in being made up of two dissimilar curves worked into one. Mr. Telford observes that it will stand comparison with any similar structure in Europe.[1]

August 30th, 1828

Made a little excursion to Sezincote, where we passed nearly two hours in viewing the house and grounds. The exterior of the former is striking and picturesque, after a Hindu model, the tomb of Hyder Ali, and the first view of the house, conservatory, flower garden, bank of wood, etc., very peculiar and pleasing; but the interior is badly arranged, and not particularly well-furnished. Several new apartments for bed chambers have recently been added; but the situation is very unfavourable under a high bank of clay covered with dense foliage, hence the house, conservatory and offices are very damp and the dry rot has already commenced its ravages. The shrubberies and drest grounds are pretty and peculiar, the oriental taste is preserved, as far as it could. Sir Charles and Lady Cockerell are now abroad.[2]

October 13th, 1828

We soon reached Cheltenham and without much difficulty found suitable and commodious lodgings in the High Street, at Mrs.

1 The design was based on Jean-Rodolphe Perronet's five-arch bridge over the Seine at Neuilly built in 1768 and its most remarkable feature is the chamfered arch. The proposed demolition of the bridge when the new bridge was opened in 1974 was defeated by the local and national conservation societies, and it has been scheduled as an Ancient Monument, and preserved.

2 Sir John Betjeman is preferable:
> 'Oxford May mornings! When the prunus bloomed
> We'd drive to Sunday lunch at Sezincote:
> First steps in learning how to be a guest,
> First wood-smoke-scented luxury of life
> In the large ambience of a country house.
> One lodge is Tudor, one in Indian style.
> The bridge, the waterfall, the Temple Pool —
> And there they burst on us, the onion domes,
> Chajjahs and chattris made of amber stone:
> Home of the oaks, exotic Sezincote!''

Maggs's, No. 345, below the Town Hall, close to the Churchyard, and nearly opposite the arcade leading into the Market. We passed the rest of the forenoon shopping and walking, being tempted by the fineness of the day to visit Pittville, and the magnificent new Pump Room, not yet completed.

October 18th, 1828

Before breakfast we joined the gay throng on the Montpellier Walk, and found a large concourse of loungers and water drinkers, considering the season of the year. In the fields beyond the Rotunda, there has sprung up this year a fine row of large and handsome houses, called Lansdowne Place or Parade, which I had never noticed before. [1]

I took a walk in the forenoon to see the progress making in two new places of worship for the Establishment. A small church or chapel behind Berkeley Place to the right of the London Road as you enter the town is the greatest readiness and will be soon pewed. [2] The Gothic church behind Montpellier, in the ground marked out for a square, to be called Suffolk Square, is much less forward, though a considerable time has elapsed since it was planned and commenced. [3] I was surprised to see the ground about this new church so little levelled or laid out for new buldings; the situation, I presume, is not popular and Suffolk Square as yet boasts but two or three finished houses; they are, however, handsome.

December 27th, 1828

The gentleman who has been appointed accountant of the Provident Bank at Stow is arrived, and entered upon his duties yesterday. This day he gave Edward a first lesson in French. Mr. Rens appears a very quiet, polite, well informed, respectable man.

1 These houses were designed by Papworth and this is the last year, 1828, he worked in Cheltenham.
2 St. John's by Papworth, now demolished.
3 St. James's finished by Papworth, and now redundant.

20th June, 1828

Non-payment of mortgage interest by Sir Thomas Phillipps likely to be pursued at law. Sir T.P., as I understand it, persists in his old expensive taste of book and manuscript collecting ....

January 9th, 1829

We had two or three guests to dinner including Mr. Rens, who returned to his lodgings in Stow. We are confirmed in our favourable opinion of him and I am glad to find that he is a Protestant.

January 12th, 1829

We left home after breakfast for Cheltenham in the close carriage, the weather being very cold and frosty. My dear wife and son proposed to convey me so far on the way to Gloucester, whither I was about to repair to attend the Epiphany Quarter Sessions; they were to return in the afternoon after shopping and a call on Lady Elcho who is now staying in Cheltenham. We found her Ladyship near Montpellier, in a shewy house, called Fancy Hall, fancifully arranged and furnished, with handsome rooms for entertaining company; but with the disadvantage of being miserably damp and cold. We were sorry to observe that her Ladyship did not derive all the amusement she expected from her removal to Cheltenham, where she had engaged this house for two months that she might enjoy more society than she could command at Stanway.

January 14th, 1829

The time of the court was entirely occupied with hearing an appeal against a conviction under the acts for the regulation of the woollen manufacturers. The question was of much importance to the great clothiers, who are very liable to be robbed by their workmen or servants of materials, which are disposed of to petty manufacturers, by whom they are worked up into cloth and kerseymere, etc. in the obscurity of their dwelling houses and petty workshops. This offence is called in the phraseology of the district *slingeing,* and from its nature is very difficult to be detected. In this present instance a great quantity of what is called waste, weaving odds and ends of yarn, was found on the premises of the accused.

Evidence all tended to the confirming of the conviction which stamped the man a *slingeer*.... and the court did indeed confirm the conviction.[1]

In the Court this forenoon I derived much pleasure from the conversation of an old acquaintance, Lord Granville Somerset, the Duke of Beaufort's second son, who came to join his father and uncle Lord Edward Somerset at Gloucester, after having brought to conclusion the Sessions at Monmouth, where his Lordship presides. He is a man of considerable talent, and very cultivated mind with an intelligent countenance and fine bald head; but sadly deformed, yet very active and a bold rider after hounds. In Parliament he is a very efficient member particularly in committees.

January 15th, 1829

I dined with the Dean *en famille*. He is at present in residence, with part only of his family at the Deanery; Mrs. Rice is at Oddington with her eldest son and most of her children; Miss Cecil and Miss Lucy Rice, with George and Henry are at Gloucester. We passed a pleasant quiet evening, the only guests besides myself being our neighbour Ford and his son from Little Rissington.

February 4th, 1829

I dined and slept at Mr. Baillie's at Great Rissington; the frost was rapidly going and the roads, which for some time had been very slippery, were now very dirty. I rode on horseback. Mr. Ford and Mr. F. Rice formed the party, the latter recently admitted to priest's orders, and presented by his father, the Dean of Gloucester, to the vicarage of Fairford. It was a remarkable piece of good fortune that this option fell to the Dean ... and he was enabled to present his son, who is an estimable and well-informed young man; but enjoying a poor share of health, and unequal without assistance to take the entire charge of a large parish with a population of between 1200 and 1500 souls.

---

1 The County historian the Rev. Thomas Dudley Fosbrooke says that in the old St. Michael's church in Gloucester there was a chantry to St. Anne, who was the patron saint for finding things lost or stolen, under the patronage of the Guild of Weavers, because slinge, or stealing wool is a common offence in clothing countries.

February 20th, 1829

I returned home. Mrs. Backhouse was somewhat better, and was taking a walk in the pleasure ground.

April 1st, 1829

The Judges came in from Monmouth and the commission was opened. Sir James Allan Park and Mr. Justice Parke, the new Judge, are on the Oxford circuit. There is likely to be a puzzle between the two Judges; but the bar has settled the difficulty by giving to the old stager, who is very religious and worthy, the name of St. James's Park, and to the new debutant that of the Green Park. The High Sheriff is Mr. Blathwayt of Dyrham Park, a young man of good fortune; his chaplain, the Rev. Mr. Robinson is clergyman of his parish and appears a pleasing young man.

April 2nd, 1829

Went to the Cathedral at 10 o'clock. A very good and pertinent sermon was preached by the Sheriff's Chaplain who adverted forcibly to the pernicious liberalism of the times, and besought the ministers of justice that they would implore the aid of divine grace to rule and direct their judgements. His discourse was a very good one and highly creditable to so young a man; one could perhaps have wished that his sentences had been couched hypothetically and generally, rather than in the first person singular. A clergyman should wait till he has been some years in the profession before he uses such sentences as begin with "I earnestly exhort", "I anxiously beseech you", "I solemnly call on you by the sacred authority with which I am invested", etc.

Since I was last in the Cathedral a monument has been erected to a pious and amiable old pastor the Rev. R. Raikes [1] brother to the Founder of the system of Sunday Schools. The monument is of stone and represents a Gothic shrine. The design is by Rickman, [2] the architect, a man of great skill and taste in the old English ecclesiastical style. He is settled at Birmingham, and is in high repute in his profession.

1 Richard Raikes, died 1823. The fact that it is by Rickman had not hitherto been noticed.
2 Thomas Rickman (1776-1841). Published a series of lectures on English styles of architecture, 1817. Invented the terms, Early English, Decorated and Perpendicular, for architectural styles, which are still used to-day.

April 28th, 1829

I walked to Over Bridge which is nearly completed. It is very beautiful, light, graceful and imposing by its span; it requires some time and consideration to convince the mind of its real dimensions. I am persuaded it will remain for centuries a testimony of the profound science of Mr. Telford. Total expense £43,269.

July 15th, 1829

I accepted an invitation from my friend Mr. Howell, who has returned from Gibraltar for some weeks to dine *en famille* and sleep at Prinknash Park, and consequently we drove out together in a chaise and reached the old mansion about 5 o'clock. My friends are now surrounded by their little people; the two boys who were left at school in England, the twins who remained behind, then just born and now nearly three years old, an infant born in Gibraltar, and a sweet little girl of six or seven years of age. No other guest but myself dined at Prinknash.

October 15th, 1829

Our friends the Howells from Prinknash arrived to pass a few days with us. The country beyond Andoversford was quite new to them. His store of anecdote, high spirits and good sense, with an inexhaustible fund of varied information, make him a most agreeable companion, and conversation never flags from lack of more interlocutors.

October 17th, 1829

A very fine day. The Howells accompanied me in the phaeton to Bourton-on-the-Water; we extended our drive as far as Little Rissington. They are agreeably surprised with the country; they had anticipated bleak hills, stone walls and all the horrors which the inhabitants of the Vale of Gloucester ascribe to the Cotswolds, and were pleased to find warm valleys, rich meadows, luxuriant hedges and a fine autumnal foliage not yet parted from the trees.

October 19th, 1829

The Howells left Upper Slaughter and I accompanied them to Prinknash Park. Part of the offices at Prinknash are under repair at present. My friend is rebuilding them exactly as they were of old. In the wall is a rude stone bas-relief of Henry VIII, who once rested here and slept, when on a progress; the royal arms are emblazoned, as was, under such circumstances, the custom. A little rude sculpture of the same King was inserted into the wall of a public house on the road to Painswick from Gloucester and in the parish of Upton, it therefore obtained the name of Harry; but the name in an agricultural district naturally enough passed over into *The Harrow*, by which appellation it continues to be called although there is the King's head painted on the sign.

October 22nd, 1829

A fine day. I left Gloucester on this occasion a day sooner than I usually do, as Stow Fair falls this year on Saturday, and at that season the tradespeople expect their bills to be paid.

November 11th, 1829

Very bad weather, yet it cleared sufficiently to enable me to ride to Great Rissington to dine with Mr. Baillie. The only other guest of my little neighbour was the Dean of Gloucester, who left us between 8 and 9 o'clock to drink tea and pass the night at Barrington Park where his brother, Lord Dynevor, is now staying with his family. I occupied the spare chamber in Baillie's nutshell of a cottage.

November 12th, 1829

Mr. Baillie accompanied me after breakfast to Stow, where the usual avocations of the Provident Bank and Justice Room detained me till a late hour when I returned home.

December 9th, 1829

The annual meeting of the Stow Provident Bank was held this day and but sparingly attended by trustees and managers; indeed the festivities of the preceding night, on which Stow Ball was held in a new and handsome room, recently erected by subscription of the gentry on the premises of the Unicorn Inn, and where more than 160 of the ball-goers of the district assembled under the presidency of Lord Edward Somerset, and the pleasures of the

chase consequent on the ball — for the Duke of Beaufort caused his
hounds to throw off at Adlestrop gate — would account for the
paucity of attendance.

January 21st, 1830

We had yesterday a very heavy fall of snow, accompanied with a
very tempestuous wind which drifted the snow as it fell and so
obstructed the roads. The fool-hardiest of the travellers today was
my neighbour Mr. Dolphin who undertook to drive his coach and
four from Lasborough, the seat of the Hon. H. Moreton,[1] five
miles beyond Tetbury, a distance of 40 miles from Eyford. He had
gone thither with his wife and her friend Miss Green on Tuesday
with two female and three male domestics, to be ready to attend a
ball given by Mr. M. at Tetbury. He was entreated to stay, but my
squire was a little wilful and started, with the addition of a couple
of cart horses to force their way through the drifts in Lasborough
Park. On the road through Tetbury, Cirencester, etc., he was more
than once forced to put cart horses in requisition; no line of road
can be more exposed. No carriage of any sort, cart or waggon had
attempted to pass along. At times the drifts of snow were so deep,
that the footboard in front of the box divided the snow like the
prow of a vessel ploughing the waves; often the hind wheels were
buried in the drifts, unable to revolve being entirely clogged with
snow, so the machine was dragged on bodily, rolling and pitching
from side to side. Much credit ought to be given to my neighbour
for consummate skill in the art, which he professes best to
understand, the art of coachmanship. Between 6 and 7 o'clock the
cavalcade had reached the purlieus of Upper Slaughter but here
their progress was inevitably stopped. To force their way through
the drifts extending to the Cheltenham road, up the hill through my
fields was beyond even Dolphin's skill and daring, and in a few
minutes the whole party, coach, horses, servants etc., came to an
anchor in my stable yard. I was summoned from my study fireside.

Not small was the confusion in the dark. Poor Mrs. D. half dead
with fright and cold, hysterical, fainting, fearing, and laughing,
crying by turns; Miss Green more collected but sadly frightened. It
was resolved that leaving the coach behind an attempt should be
made to reach Eyford on foot. Wine and biscuits and the warmth
of a good fire renovated the drooping strength and spirits of the

1 Afterwards 2nd Earl of Ducie.

ladies. The gala cloaks and muffs were left behind; my ladies equipped their friends in wraps of humbler pretensions but better calculated to face the inclemency of the night. We later learned with satisfaction the group had safely reached home.

February 7th, 1830

Charity has been very generally and liberally extended towards the suffering lower classes, nor was it ever more wanted; for fuel has been extremely scarce and dear, owing to the canals being frozen; at Stow coals have been selling at fifty shillings per ton, the ordinary price being about twenty eight shillings.

March 8th, 1830

Mrs. Backhouse returned to us from Gloucester to-day after a visit to the fair city, which was intended only to last a fortnight, and has been prolonged to more than five weeks.

April 14th, 1830

I met a party of my Clerical brethren to-day at dinner at Stow, this being the first meeting for the season of the Stow Clerical Society. Fourteen gentlemen dined together; the Dean of Gloucester in the chair. The Dean brought with him a gentleman who has for some time resided at Oddington in the joint capacity of curate there and tutor to the Dean's younger sons. This young man is imbued with what are called Evangelical principles, not in a less degree I believe than his compeer, Baillie at Great Rissington, and as such both are in high favour with the influential lady, Mrs. Dean who with one, if not more of her daughters, has of late adopted puritanical views with great zeal; labouring to convert the good Dr. Rice, who has not yet embraced the new doctrines to the full extent, though, apparently somewhat warped towards them. How far the females of the family have succeeded with the eldest son, the incumbent of Fairford, I know not; probably he will yield soon, if he has not already succumbed, as his wife, a sister of his parishioner Mr. Raymond-Barker, is strongly biased in the same way; moreover his curate, a youth recommended from Wadham College, is reported to hold similar opinions.

Gatcombe Park

April 20th, 1830

The new High Sheriff is David Ricardo, a magistrate, of Gatcombe Park,[1] near Minchinhampton, second son of the wealthy political economist of that name, now deceased, whose theories of finance have so blindly been followed in the adjustment of the currency, to the great injury, as is alleged, of the country.

April 20th, 1830

A rumour was whispered that the new bridge at Over had given way and was in danger of falling. Mr. Telford was called upon to report on the security of the structure.

Howell and I walked to the Gloucester and Berkeley Canal basin, now crowded with vessels, many of them of large size, and presenting a busy scene. Capacious warehouses are already finished and occupied on one side and a large range is in progress of erection in another quarter. It is astonishing how much the trade of the port and canal have increased, beyond the most sanguine expectations. The exports of salt for foreign ports and the fisheries are on a very large scale; the iron manufactures are largely exported through this channel and a great quantity of corn, chiefly from Ireland, is imported. A considerable trade in timber, principally from our North American colonies, is carried on; even Liverpool receives from hence, by canal, large quantities of timber. Slates are a principle article brought from Wales for use in the inland ports. Two houses in the wine trade make large importations from Spain and Portugal; to these may be added wool, barilla, etc.

30th April, 1830

Early after breakfast Mr. Rens (the accountant of the Stow Provident Bank, and Edward's French tutor) and I set out for Cheltenham. The morning was passed in walking about to the gratification of my friend, who, though he had formed a very favourable idea of Cheltenham from the descriptions which he had heard, found the reality to exceed his anticipations. It was a *belle*

---

1 Gatcombe Park was built c. 1770 for Edward Sheppard, a gentleman, whose son sold it in 1814 to David Ricardo, M.P. the political economist. Ricardo employed George Basevi to do work here c. 1820, and Gatcombe presents an appearance unaltered since then, as even the Conservatory was there in 1829. The stables are built round a polygonal yard with an embattled wall facing the buildings. The Queen bought the house from Lord Butler in 1976 for Princess Anne.

ville, Londres en miniature, des superbes boutiques, des promenades magnifiques etc. In fact to a stranger it is an interesting and exciting place; the town and country are so happily combined, gay equipages, well-dressed people, riding, driving, and walking about, the bustle of the street, and the liveliness of the scene are calculated to attract. In the evening we took a pleasant walk in the fields to Sandford.

May 1st, 1830

We all went to the walks before breakfast visiting the Imperial, Montpellier and Old Spas. After brea fast we drove to the Pittville Walks and Pump-room; no great prc ress has been made in the buildings in this quarter; indeed the other side of the town is the preferable and more fashionable quarter, and it is said that large speculations are meditated in the vicinity of Bay's Hill Lodge. Already there is behind the Montpellier Pump-room a splendid row of houses of the first class called Lansdown Place, in front of which passes the new road to Gloucester, which is now open for travelling. Behind Lansdown Place it is proposed to erect a number of streets, squares, etc. But at Pittville all is comparatively still, although the situation is very attractive, the walks and drives and sheet of water are all laid out with much taste and judgement and on a grand scale, corresponding with the Pump-room, which is a magnificent and costly edifice, nearly complete, but not yet opened. It is a truly superb temple of Hygeia with colonnade, dome, pillars, highly finished architectural ornaments, especially as regards the dome and ceiling. A splendid marble and scagliola pump and appendages have been recently erected.

The spirited proprietor and projector, Mr. Pitt, my old acquaintance, M.P. for Cricklade, who in the course of a long life has risen from the lowest rank in society to wealth and consequence, must, I fear, find this an unprofitable concern, less advantageous than if the money it has cost had been invested in 3% annuities. It is expected that the whole will be leased out to some speculators not averse to run some risk, and that the opening of the room will not be much longer delayed. My wife who had joined us with Mr. Rens on foot, took a seat in the Phaeton to return into the town with her mother and myself.

Making a call, shopping and walking in the High Street occupied the rest of the morning till we sat down to an early dinner, after which Mr. Rens and myself were to return to Upper Slaughter. The First of May was duly observed; the Floralia were kept with grotesque mummery, dancing and masquerading by the chimney sweepers, who wandered about collecting pence and carrying ambulatory bowers and rude garlands, while the public coaches, and musicians playing on the bugle.

As we drove out of the town about 5 o'clock in the afternoon, the first London coach came in gallantly, greeted by a large concourse of people in the streets. Later in the evening the coaches were driven in procession through the principal streets. My neighbour Dolphin, who is now staying in Cheltenham joined the procession with his coach and team driven by himself. Gentlemen and even ladies graced it both within and on the roof: this may be fashionable, but it is more honoured in the breach than in the observance, and the whole system of the "four in hand" is unworthy of an English country gentleman and man of fortune. While these vagaries were enacted, we had given folly the go-by, and were travelling homewards; both Rens and myself enjoyed a refreshing dish of tea after our arrival at the Rectory.

May 10th, 1830

I attended the Archdeacon of Gloucester's visitation at Stow. The sermon was preached by Mr. Cornelius Pitt, Rector of Hazelton and curate of Notgrove. He had borrowed his discourse from Gilpin.[1] By many among our country clergy the composition of original sermons is far too much neglected;disuse begets distrust of one's own powers, and a disinclination to the labour. Mr. Pitt is a shrewd, intelligent man and quite equal to the composition of a plain discourse on Christian doctrines ... He is the eldest son of Mr. Pitt (of Pittville). By marrying a widow, Mrs. Robins, he disobliged his father although there was nothing discreditable in the connection; the lady lacked wealth but was highly estimable. The father withdrew his favour from Cornelius and left him to struggle through life with very inadequate means. This disagreement induced the son to go into the church, and the income to be derived from a curacy was better than nothing. As curate of Chedworth he cultivated Lord Stowell's good will, who considered him to have been unfairly treated and procured for him from his brother, the Lord Chancellor Eldon, the living of Hazelton.

1 William Gilpin (1724-1804), published Lectures on Church Catechism,, Exposition of the New Testament' 1790, and five works describing his summer· tours.

James Henry Monk Bishop of Gloucester

A charge was then delivered by the Archdeacon which lasted nearly, if not quite an hour. Dr. Timbrill observes the same sonorous cadence, whether he is speaking of the higher topics of religious faith, or ministerial duty, or the *flocci, nauci, nihili, pili,* the duties of the churchwardens, repairs of the fabric, pews, right of sit tings, hassocks, and the like.A large party of the clergy then dined together, including the Dean of Gloucester, and Dr. Twisleton, for my neighbour at Adlestrop has proceeded to the degree of LLD as he tells us, that he may be able to oblige his friends at New College, by giving a vote at Oxford in the Convocation house — at the same time he deprecates being addressed by his acquaintance as Doctor.

June 13th, 1830

Dr. Monk,[1] the Dean of Peterborough, is at last gazetted as Bishop of Gloucester.

April 18th, 1832

The Reform Bill has passed the second reading in the House of Lords. The votes were for the second reading 184, against it 175; majority 9. The Bishop of Gloucester maintained his opinions against the measure with more firmness and boldness than I had anticipated. It required some nerve in Dr. Monk to detach himself from his Cambridge friends (Kaye, Bishop of Lincoln, and Blomfield, Bishop of London). A strong temptation was to be resisted by a junior bishop, the holder of a poor see; but it seems that Dr. Monk is not devoid of firmness and vindicated his views with judgement, and answered with much spirit a very intemperate attack which the violent Popish peer the Earl of Shrewsbury had made on the episcopal order, whom he denounced as the enemies of liberty. From what I had seen of him (the Bishop) I was led to regard him as a learned Greek, but incautious, injudicious and precipitate. What I have seen and heard of him in his diocese does not pre-possess me in his favour.[2]

---

1 James Henry Monk, born 1784. Bishop of Gloucester 1830-6 and of Gloucester and Bristol 1836 — till his death in 1856.
2 Witts was a Tory, and suspicious of reform; but thought a clergyman should not be prominent in political contentions. His opinion of his diocesan improved with the years.

March 7th, 1832. Ash Wednesday

Attended the services at the parish church (Cheltenham). Mr. Close[1] is incumbent, a person extremely popular with the serious party, of a pleasing exterior, in middle life, possessing the natural advantage of a fine voice. The evening sermon was by Mr. Close, an hour in length, preached to a very large and attentive congregation, the church being lighted by gas. Of the lower orders there was a large proportion — a gratifying sight; many elegant females of the higher order were assembled. The preacher is decidedly eloquent and impressive and appeared to deliver his lecture extempore, referring to a Bible, which he took into the pulpit and which probably contained copious notes.

March 29th, 1832

Mr. Canning of Hartpury, near Gloucester, is High Sheriff, a Roman Catholic gentleman and the first of his persuasion, who has held the office in this county. He is a popular man among the Whigs, a *bon-vivant* and an old sportsman; but served the office sadly against his will, and in a shabby manner with a mean looking carriage and horses and homely liveries, etc. He was bigotted enough to decline accompanying the judges into the cathedral this morning; but left them at the gate, returning to take them up and convey them in his carriage to the court.

January 18th, 1833

We dined at Lady Reade's at Oddington, a party of seventeen. Sir John Reade's birthday: who was present. Sir Charles and Lady Imhoff, Miss Chapuset, a Col. and Mrs. Willard, on a visit to Lady R. agreeable people of the world, Mr. Wynniatt, his eldest son and daughter, Mr. Chamberlayne with ourselves made up the party. Dinner at half-past six (seven) o'clock: lamps lighted in our carriage to go to Oddington: cold raw weather and thick fog: home at a quarter past one o'clock. Our fathers were more sensible, who kept earlier hours, and visited when the moon was bright.

---

1 Francis Close (1797-1882) evangelical divine, rector of Cheltenham 1826, Dean of Carlisle 1856.

January 21st, 1833

Dined at Mrs. Hasting's, Daylesford House. Met nearly the same people as we did on Friday at Oddington.

February 1st, 1833

We dined at Mr. Leigh's at Broadwell and met Sir Charles and Lady Imhoff, Miss Chapuset, Mr. and Mrs. Vavasour of Stow, Messrs. W.B. and Mundy Pole; with the family party we sat down fifteen to dinner. Music in the evening, the Misses Leigh playing and singing. It was a cold evening for a drive: moonlight, but not frosty; remains of snow, which had fallen yesterday, lingered on the roads. The Reform Parliament assembled on Tuesday.

April 8th, 1833

After an early breakfast we left home in our close carriage. It was past 8 o'clock when we got to Cirencester, where we found the town extremely crowded, it being a fair. We changed horses there and in an hour (10 miles) reached Tetbury as solitary as Cirencester had been full of bustle. Soon after the Cross Hands we saw Dodington, the seat of Sir Bethell Codrington, a fine park and well wooded, occupying the side of the hills and the mansion[1] a very extensive pile of building, environed with stables, gardens, and the usual accompaniments of a wealthy country gentleman. Codrington is a large West India proprietor but has great estates in Gloucestershire.

Passing through the village of Sodbury, we came to the market town of Chipping Sodbury, an old, *triste* and deserted-looking place. Here the aspect of the country is uninteresting, pastured by ragged horses and donkeys and geese, and bordered by mean-looking cottages, half dilapidated and a general air of discomfort prevailed. The country is indeed more populous than our Cotswold hills; but the people have a less rural cast, being chiefly colliers or engaged in the hat and other manufactories. One tract of common over which we passed is called Coalpitheath, a ragged-looking spot, people and their dwellings being all out at elbows. As we drew nearer to Bristol the country improved ....

1 c. 1810 by James Wyatt.

September, 1833

To Toddington where Mr. Eddy was kind enough to be our guide to see Mr. Tracy's splendid house. The family still occupy apartments in what remains of the old house, but pass most of the day in the new one. Entered the dress-ground through the pheasantry, which is very well arranged in an umbrageous corner; here the trees, walks and lawns are well grouped, affording an enjoyable promenade and a striking view of the most enriched front of the building, all scrupulously antique in the style of architecture ... with Gothic windows. The Gothic door is at the termination of a series of arches as at Lichfield Cathedral; on one side is the Knight de Tracy with his weapon in a menacing attitude and on the other Thomas à Beckett shrinking from the impending blow. On the front are a full length statue of Henry VIII the dissolver of monastries, and statues of monks, done by workmen on the spot under the superintendance of Mr. Tracy, an accomplished amateur architect.

Entering by the principal door, we came into a cloister imitated from Magdalen College, Oxford; with it all the apartments communicate. The space between the arches is fitted up with painted glass windows purchased by Mr. Tracy in Switzerland, Swabia, etc. Very curious and admirably executed, containing coats of arms, figures etc; what was deficient has been supplied by the skill of a celebrated artist in painted glass at Shrewsbury. On the other side of the cloisters is an unfinished billiard room, intended to be fitted up with ancient carving, after the model of a piece of antique wood carving, brought from Hailes, in high preservation, which is to be placed over the chimney piece. Once elegant painted window lights the staircase filled with ancient painted glass, being a window purchased by Mr. Tracy from a church in France.

October 14th, 1833

Received a letter from Howell from Prinknash; he shortly enters on his western tour to visit the manufacturers, in his new character of Inspector of Factories.

October 15th, 1833. Cheltenham

Walked to Pittville, where we were, as non-subscribers, admitted on the payment of one shilling. The place is very well kept, the walks in excellent order and the shrubberies very much grown, and all the gardens very luxuriant. Though but a few individuals were in the splendid Pumproom, a small band of musicians, playing on wind instruments, performed many pleasing pieces of music. In the reading room was exposed for sale (fifty guineas was asked) a curious piece of ancient wood carving, said to have been originally brought from the church at Earls Croome, Worcestershire, where, it was added, it may be traced for 700 years. As to the antiquity I have my doubts, but certainly it is a curious relic, representing various scenes in our Saviour's history.

October 16th, 1833

Walked before breakfast to the Montpellier Walks and Spa where we found even at this season a numerous company of water drinkers and promenaders. Met Mr. George who had attended the Sessions at Gloucester yesterday, and told me that Mr. Bathurst of Lydney Park has been appointed Chairman. It had been rumoured that the Whig party would have proposed some magistrate of their own politics; but as they would have had little chance in a court the majority of whose members hold Tory opinions it was prudent of them not to make the trial. Mr. Bathurst was brought up at the bar, is a sound lawyer, a very steady, upright, grave man. When I was last at the Quarter Sessions a most unjustifiable attack on the clerical magistrates was made by that hot headed, ill conditioned veteran Whig, Colonel Kingscote. That might have passed; but not a single voice was raised by a solitary layman present to disavow the insulting language used against the clergy, and I have felt little disposition to expose myself to a fresh insult. I more than doubt the wisdom in the present excited state of the country of a clergyman appearing at the Quarter Sessions; the contention between Whig and Tory runs high. [1]

1 There is an Ackerman print of 1833 after Alken called "Hunting versus Reform", or "the Sporting Sweep" or "To tell you the truth, Gemmen, I can't vote for you, 'cause I 'unts with the Duke". The text is as follows:— "At Chipping Sodbury in Gloucestershire, resides a certain chimney-sweep, who by industry has accumulated some property. He happens, however to be very fond of the chase and is often seen with the Duke of Beaufort's hounds to the great amusement of the gentlemen, amongst whom however he never fails to maintain a conspicuous place. The sweep is a Reformer, but the Duke's brother Lord Edward Somerset is a candidate for one division of the county on opposite principles. The sweep was consequently rather puzzled as to the disposal of his vote. The Reform candidates were the first to put him to the test, understanding that his political creed was favourable they solicited his vote. To their surprise the sweep refused them saying "To tell you the truth, gemmen, I can't vote for you 'cause I 'unts with the Duke".

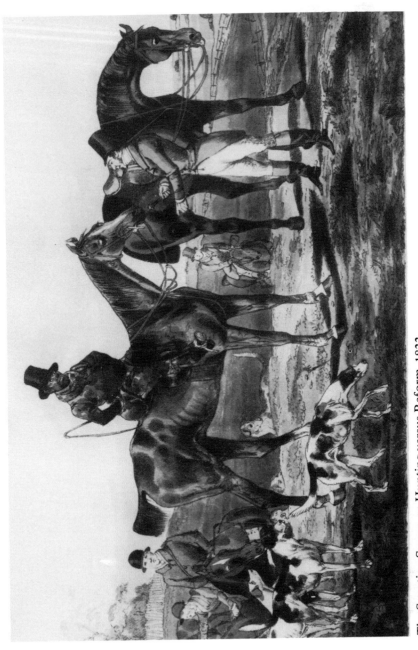

March 13th, 1834

We learnt with great grief the melancholy news of the murder of our worthy friend F.J. Rens, actuary of the Stow Provident Bank. The story was a blind one; but I fear correct in the main. The horrible deed appears to have been perpetrated by some desperate vagrants near Stow, who attacked the poor old man while taking a walk. For many months the roads have swarmed with sturdy and ferocious looking vagabonds. A foreigner, decayed in circumstances, living in banishment from his country, Rens has endeared himself to high and low in the neighbourhood of Stow.

March 14th, 1834

It appears that Rens was waylaid on Monday evening last at half past seven, as he returned from a walk, by three ruffians near the horsepool at Stow, who robbed him of his gold watch and purse and beat his brains out. It does not appear what steps were taken to detect the murderers, or that there was any prospect of their apprehension.

July 26th, 1834

Rode to Stow to investigate the outrageous conduct of three wandering American sailors, who besides being vagrants had been demanding goods and money with menaces and force at various villages and farmhouses in the neighbourhood. On clear evidence we (the magistrates) agreed that these ruffians, fellows half naked, ferocious, exquisitely blackguard and insolent, should be committed for trial at the Michaelmas Sessions, though the case at Condicote fell to the ground through the unwillingness of the farmer's wife to swear that she was intimidated. This being the day of the Stow wool-fair, and the appearance and conduct of the prisoners, together with their violent resistance on being apprehended by the police, having attracted much attention, the Justice room was crowded during the proceedings.

The enquiry respecting the murder of Mr. Rens being thus deferred we were detained till half past nine o'clock in examining witnesses, dining at the White Hart with the other magistrates. The evening proved very rainy and it was between ten and eleven when my son and myself returned home, enclosed in borrowed garments.

Saintbridge House

August 11th, 1834

After breakfast left home with my son in our open carriage with our groom, for Northleach to vote for Codrington (Tory Parliamentary candidate); to-day and to-morrow being fixed for the poll. Everything went on with good humour. On the Blue side, James Dutton, Lord Sherborne's eldest son, was conspicuous maintaining a cause opposite to that espoused by his father. At a little past 12 Edward and I pursued our course toward Prinknash Park, baiting at Frogmill Inn, where I met Mrs. Browne and her elder daughter taking a drive, and had a parley with them. Edward botanized. At 2 we set forward again by Cubberley, the Air Balloon at the top of Crickley Hill, Birdlip and Todd's Cottages to Prinknash where we arrived at half past 4 and were kindly welcomed by our excellent friends Mr. and Mrs. Howell whom we found surrounded by their fine family of children and no other guests besides ourselves. In the evening William Howell who had been at Gloucester and dined with the Wintles at Saintbridge, came home and reported that Codrington had a large majority on the poll there at the close of the day.

August 12th, 1834

Brilliant but scorching weather. After an early breakfast drove with my son to Gloucester. Howell did not accompany us. His position as holding office under the present government dictates to him the propriety of neutrality in contested elections for the county. Drove to Spa Hotel, as a quiet place out of the bustle of the election. The polling was proceeding at the hustings in Eastgate Street, and though many were sanguine that the Blues would succeed, much anxiety was felt by the partizans of the Tory party, even to the close of the poll. The respective parties mustered when the poll was over at their headquarters, the Bell Hotel being the Blue house and the King's Head the yellow. Before the mob dispersed we left Gloucester for Prinknash. At night came a hurried and hardly intelligible note to me of the victory gained by the Blues, Codrington having a majority. Thus the Tory principles have triumphed once more, the Whig Ministerial candidate being rejected.

August 14th, 1834

A brilliant summer's day. Took a sauntering walk with Howell through the beech woods to the beautifully situated village of

Cranham at the head of the valley of Painswick, and near the source of the Stroudwater which turns the wheels of the greater part of the mills of the Gloucestershire clothing district. This sequestered hamlet contains more than one pottery for the manufacture of coarse earthenware, such as garden pots, milk pans, earthenware pipes, etc. Looked into one of the potteries where the process was going forward: rude turning lathes at work. The master and his men bore striking marks of the practical zeal with which the Blue interest had been supported: black eyes and a broken nose disfigured the potters, master and men. Mr. Lovegrove, the potter, acted as our Cicerone to the church, a neat ancient building placed on a knoll overlooking the rich valley and backed by magnificient beech woods. A stranger would suppose the place to be a peaceful, innocent, rural abode of good will and honest simplicity; but Cranham has no resident gentleman or clergyman and the habits of the people are thievish and gross. Gypsies are abounding at all seasons in the woods. The potters, besides being a quarrelsome race, have little regard for *meum* and *tuum*. The living is in the gift of Mrs. Pitt of Gloucester and is held with the adjoining benefice of Brimpsfield. Edward accompanied us part of the way to Cranham; but left us to pursue his favourite study of botany in the woods.

August 15th, 1834

Mrs. Howell, Emmeline and William set out before breakfast to pass the day at Cheltenham and attend a concert. A clergyman of the name of Parker, incumbent of a Pembroke College living in Suffolk, called before breakfast to ask leave to see the house, and prospect from the terrace. He was staying with Mr. Wintle at Saintbridge and appeared a worthy man, strongly bitten with a taste for antiquarian and architectural research. After breakfast Edward set off on one of Howell's ponies to Gloucester. Howell, Mr. Parker and myself followed in the phaeton. We drove to the Spa Hotel. To-day was devoted to the chairing of the new member, exuberant joy and feasting. Repaired to the Bell Hotel. A great mob of nobility, gentry, clergy and commonalty were congregated, all profusely decked with blue favours, while a host of fair ladies occupied the front windows of the hotel. The great attraction was the arrival of a procession from Cheltenham, the way being led by the father of the successful candidate, Sir Bethell Codrington and his lady, followed by Sir William Hicks, an octogenarian who had voted at the great county contest between Chester and Berkeley in

1776. Many were the county gentlemen with whom I mingled in conversation, among them the handsome hero of the day, of whom it were to be wished that his talent and habits of business equalled the enthusiasm of his adherents. A splendid blue chair had been provided, Codrington looked and acted the part well; as there was no occasion to make a speech, in which he is not an adept, there was nothing to detract from the occasion. I accompanied the triumphal march down Westgate Street and part of the way back, when I retired, nearly overcome by the pressure, heat, noise and dust. Then I sauntered about with Edward and others, sometimes resorting to the Bell.

August 16th, 1834

Left our kind friends the Howells to return to Upper Slaughter. Edward prolonged his visit but accompanied me as far as Todd's Cottages, where he left to explore the beech woods in search of plants, and to visit the Roman Villa at Witcombe.

August 22nd, 1834

Left home in the open carriage with my servant, and arrived to breakfast at Cheltenham. Found my wife and her mother in comfortable lodgings at the end of the Colonnade. Received a call from Under-Secretary Backhouse, who is staying in Cheltenham with his family. While they were with us, arrived our friends from Prinknash Park and my son Edward. In the evening went to the Montpellier Spa and enjoyed the music greatly, such as the Hallelujah Chorus, the Overture to Cenerentola, *Gratias agimas* by Guglielmi, etc. The musicians wore blue *surtouts* with a crimson sash and blue cloth caps with silver band and tassel. Till the twilight came on the performances were without doors at the head of the principal walk under the portico of the Pump Room. Afterwards the band moved into the Rotunda.

August 23rd, 1834

A fine day with the exception of a shower about 2 o'clock. Before breakfast went to the promenade on the Well Walk, where we were joined by our cousins the Backhouses. About 9 o'clock the band struck up the National Anthem which announced the presence of the Duke of Gloucester, who is now making his annual

The Duke of Gloucester

séjour at Cheltenham. The prince, who loves to display here his connection with Royalty, advanced through the Pump Room to the head of the walk. He afterwards entered into conversation with such of his acquantiance as he deigned to select. He is aged in appearance, vacant in countenance; but retains a princely air, with a strong family resemblance to his Royal race. Two of his equerries joined our party, and the Duke singled out Backhouse to walk with him.

At one o'clock arrived the Prinknash party, Mr. and Mrs. Howell, Emmeline, Laura, Constance, and Edward in a fly and William on his pony, whom we accompanied to a temporary circus to witness an exhibition of horsemanship and the like.

September 14th, 1834
Duke of Gloucester's death.[1]

1 The Dukedom of Gloucester.
I.	1385-1397. Thomas of Woodstock, Duke of Gloucester son of King Edward III.
II.	1414-1447. Humphrey of Lancaster, Duke of Gloucester son of King Henry IV and Mary de Bohun. Called "Good Duke Humphrey". Founder of Library at Oxford.
III.	1461-1485. Richard Plantaganet, Duke of Gloucester son of Richard Duke of York and Cecily Neville, became King Richard III.
IV.	1640-1660. Henry Stuart, Duke of Gloucester son of King Charles I. Died aged 20.
V.	1689-1700. Prince William, Duke of Gloucester, son of Queen Anne. Died aged 12.
VI.	1714(?)-1726. Prince Frederick Lewis, Prince of Wales, son of King George II.
VII.	1764. Prince William Henry, Duke of Gloucester, third son of Frederick, Prince of Wales.
VIII.	1805-1834. Prince William Frederick, Duke of Gloucester, son of above, born 15th January 1776 and married his first cousin the Princess Mary fourth daughter of King George III. Honours extinct. Their only daughter Princess Mary Adelaide married the Duke of Teck and became the mother of Queen Mary, and grandmother of Mary, Duchess of Beaufort.
IX.	1928. Prince Henry, Duke of Gloucester, son of King George V and Queen Mary. Born 1900, married Lady Alice Montagu-Douglas-Scott daughter of 7th Duke of Buccleuch.
X.	1975. Prince Richard, Duke of Gloucester, second and surviving son of Prince Henry and Princess Alice, Duchess of Gloucester. H.R.H. is ninth in line of accession to the throne, and his son the Earl of Ulster tenth.

December 2nd, 1834

Dispatched a packet with a letter to the Bishop of Gloucester, containing Mr. Lawrence's little pamphlet on the management of cottage gardens, with a copy of the rules on which the Allotment system is here conducted. His Lordship proposes this autumn to assign a few acres of land close to Gloucester to poor families to be cultivated by spade husbandry.

December 21st, 1834
(See May 13, 1835)

The Gloucestershire Chronicle announces that Mr. Hyett has withdrawn from the representation of the Borough of Stroud. He declares that he is induced so to do solely on private grounds and I think it probable that, with a large young family and moderate fortune, he is acting prudently, but as he was partial to the pursuits of a legislator and a man of more than average talent, I cannot but suspect that he is actuated by a conviction, which I have heard him privately express, that the Liberal party to which he has attached himself, had carried their principles too far, and that the time was come to endeavour to return to more Conservative principles and measures. As member for a borough where radical opinions abound and a system of dictation is organized, he would have found it very difficult to detach himself from violent men and rash projects.

April 13th, 1835

A frosty morning, followed by a fine day. Rose at ½ past 3 a.m. breakfast at 4; left home at ½ past 4 for Gloucester with my son in the phaeton to Cheltenham, where we arrived at 7 o'clock, and took a fly to Gloucester, where we arrived at 8 o'clock and took a second breakfast at the Bell Hotel.

By ½ past 8 my son and myself entered the Criminal Court, together with the Judge and the High Sheriff (H.W. Newman Esq.), and obtained very good seats on the Bench. With Edmund Jeffrey was arraigned a person of the name of Forbes,[1] late an architect at Cheltenham, charged with forgery. He pleaded not guilty: not so Edmund Jeffrey, who in a steady tone pleaded guilty to his indictment. Mr. Justice Coleridge, in a very persuasive

1 John Forbes, the distinguished architect of the Pittville Pumproom.

Monday Apr. 13.

A frosty morning, followed by a fine day.

Rose at half past three A.M.: breakfast at four o'clock, left home at half past four for Gloucester with my son in the Phaeton to Cheltenham, where we arrived at seven o'clock; one took a fly to Gloucester, where we arrived at eight o'clock, and took a second breakfast at the Bell Hotel:

By half past eight my son and myself entered the Crown in a Court together with the Judge and High Sheriff, and obtained very good seats on the Bench. H.E. Edmund Jeffrey was arraigned, a person of the name of Forster, late an architect at Cheltenham—dissipated work. Jeffrey.

He pleaded not guilty, ... to Edmund Jeffrey, who in a steady tone replied. guilty to his indictment. Mr Justice Coleridge, in a very persuasive manner cautioned him as to the file he had taken, that notice; explained to him that if any one had advised him to that course he had been ill advised,

Facsimile of entry for April 13 1835

John Forbes

manner cautioned him as to the plea he had thus put in; explained to him that if anyone had advised him to that course he had been ill-advised: that no one would think more unfavourably of him for pleading Not Guilty: that to plead guilty would be no benefit to him either here or hereafter, and explained to him in the usual manner the legal gloss put on the plea Not Guilty. The poor youth seemed fully to apprehend him, and after a little hesitation retracted his former plea. I own, I greatly doubt the propriety of the course usually adopted from the bench on such occasions and was not sorry to find that even experienced counsellors partook of my feeling: at such a time when the conviction of the magnitude of the crime is full in the culprit's mind, when he has brought himself to confess, surely it is wrong by sophisticated argument, however dictated by merciful and charitable feeling, that something may yet interpose between the cup and the lip, to revive the abandoned hope of acquital, and suggest a deliberate lie to the poor wretch who trembles on the verge of eternity.

Before, however, taking the case of murder, that of forgery was selected for trial, in order to release Serjeant Ludlow who was retained for the defence of Forbes, ... the sooner to draw to a close the business of this protracted Assize. Forbes had long lived in credit at Cheltenham in the pursuit of his profession; had been engaged there in very important works; had been the architect employed in the erection of Pittville, both the Pump-room and the handsome residences on that property, also had built St. Paul's Church. But he had connected himself with a person of the name of Prosser in building speculations, and had engaged with him in a series of bill transactions of a temporizing character, such as in a moral view are barely removed from a fraud, though so generally resorted to and connived at in an unsound state of trade. Prosser had certainly permitted Forbes, indeed had authorized him to accept bills for him by subscribing the name of the former; Forbes had, however, gone one step too far, and to supply his own necessities, certainly on one occasion, and there is little doubt on more than one, had negotiated a bill for a sum between £20 and £30 with Prosser's acceptance, his signature being imitated, but without his knowledge. This bill paid by Forbes to a butcher of the name of Brunsdon, and cashed by him, the butcher retaining the amount of his bill for meat against Forbes, was that on which the allegation of forgery was raised. Prosser and Brunsdon were examined for the prosecution, and most tryingly cross examined by Serjeant Ludlow for the defence; and, undoubtedly the facts elicited by that able counsel exhibited Mr. Prosser in a most unfavourable light, and displayed in disgusting detail the whole of the unprincipled system of accommodation bills. But however the Jury might have been disposed to discredit Prosser as to the fact of the particular bill in question being an unsanctioned forgery, further evidence of a most condemnatory nature was produced, even a letter written by the prisoner, while in gaol, which amounted to an admission that the bill in question as well as others were fraudulent. And though a host of most respectable witnesses, old and highly creditable inhabitants of Cheltenham, flocked into Court to bear testimony to the general excellence and integrity of Forbes's character, the Jury after a long deliberation found the unhappy man guilty, and sentence of transportation for life was pronounced in a most feeling and impressive manner by the Judge. This trial excited the deepest interest among the inhabitants of Cheltenham, the character of Prosser received perhaps a fatal blow; and there is little doubt that a successful effort will be made to obtain for Forbes a commutation of the sentence into imprisonment for a comparatively short term of years. ¹ (And this indeed proved to be the case though poor Forbes disappears from view.)

And now came the trial of Edmund Jeffrey. Mr. Alexander and Mr. Cripps were engaged for the prosecution and Mr. Greaves for the prisoner. Both Alexander and Greaves conducted the affair with great skill and judgement. Mr. Rogers, who saw Mr. Rens go out on his last walk, and knew that he took his watch with him, was examined. But the gist of the case lay in the confessions of the wretched youth, particularly in the first made before Mr. Ford in Northleach and to prove which the Keeper of the Bridewell there and Ford were examined. The Keeper hesitated a good deal, when it was pressed upon him in cross examination that he had held out inducements to the prisoner to confess when he went into his cell to inform him that Mr. Ford wanted to see him. Mr. Ford (the magistrate) also hesitated when cross examined. He admitted he had not cautioned the prisoner that what he disclosed would be evidence against him. On this Mr. Greaves argued very earnestly that the confession was not freely given and the magistrate had

---

1 Bryan Little in his book *Cheltenham in Pictures* (David & Charles, 1967), says on p. 51 "papers at the College show that in 1842 Forbes was still working in the town". This confirms my belief that he only went to prison for a couple of years, or so. *The Strangers Guide* in 1832 refers to him as J. Forbes Esquire, an architect of Cheltenham, and as "a gentleman". Before Witts's eye-witness account of the trial came to light, nobody seems to have known of the awful fate that overwhelmed him. Bryan Little shows a picture of Forbes as well as one of Pitt on this page.

withheld the warning till the miserable youth had already declared himself the murderer ... The learned Judge stated that in his opinion the doctrine of cautioning parties charged with crimes might be carried too far, that the object was to elicit truth, and that guilty persons ought not to be checked in the inclination to confess by an over scrupulous adherence to a punctilious rule ... The confession taken down by Mr. Ford was then read in evidence. The Judge then suggested that all which could now be brought forward would only be repetition and it would be desirable here to close the case. The charge to the Jury was conceived in the most solemn, calm and impressive spirit; there was little if any deliberation and a verdict of guilty was returned. The learned Judge after a few moments of rumination put on the awful black cap and never was heard a more feeling, beautiful and solemn address than that which he made to the wretched culprit. I sat directly opposite the unhappy youth — his countenance as usual was heavy and inexpressive — for the most part he exhibited great fortitude, but at one moment I discovered strong marks of internal agitation, his bosom heaved, his whole frame was for an instant convulsed; but he quickly resumed his self-possession and made a respectful motion of acquiescence to his sentence which purported that his hours were numbered and that on Wednesday morning he would be led to the scaffold. As to the watch, no difficulty was made in delivering it to me that it might be forwarded to the family of the murdered Mr. Rens.

The trial was not concluded till 3 p.m. and after I left the Court I walked about for half an hour with my son to calm the agitation of my spirits before I joined my colleagues Bathurst and Baker who had already for some time been engaged in auditing the County accounts. Edward shortly afterwards left Gloucester for Prinknash Park in conformity with a note from our friend Howell which had met us on our arrival at Gloucester this morning.

After two hours labour with Bathurst and Baker I retired to the Bell to dinner and continued to prepare for the business of to-morrow till midnight. It had been a harassing and eventful day, my mind had been on the stretch as it were, for twenty hours, when I retired to rest.

April 14th, 1835

Repaired before breakfast to the Gaol to confer with the Chaplain on the importance of ascertaining from Edmund Jeffrey whether he really had any accomplice. The Chaplain told me that

Jeffrey expressed his apprehension that in yielding to the Judge, and withdrawing his plea of Guilty he had committed a grievous offence. This shows a sensibility of conscience which induces the hope that his heart has been truly touched by the grace of God. Jeffrey had admitted he had an accomplice. I was accosted by Jeffrey's mother ... she spoke in a language of the sect to which she has attached herself, the Wesleyan Methodists; but with calmness and self possession. We pressed her to influence the young man to a full disclosure. This painful interview detained me long and I afterwards went to breakfast at the Bell Hotel.

The Quarter Sessions began. Charles Bathurst in the Chair. Attended in the Grand Jury Room ...

April 15th, 1835

The execution of poor Edmund Jeffrey took place this forenoon.[1] It proved impossible for the chaplain to extract anything from the miserable man as to the suspicion that he had an accomplice. He underwent the extreme penalty of the law with great firmness and decorum; he addressed the assembled crowds at some length, warning them against bad associations, sabbath breaking and frequenting beer houses.

April 16th, 1835

A very cold morning. Edward and I left our kind Prinknash friends about one o'clock by the Bath coach for Cheltenham, where we found our phaeton awaiting us and returned to Upper Slaughter, to dinner.

May 13th, 1835

Howell confirms what has already been hinted in the newspapers, that Lord John Russell will at length be seated in the House of Commons for the District borough of Stroud. This will be a curious exemplification of the working of the Reform Bill. A popular ministry, as it is alleged, is formed by the Whigs. The

---

1 In one year 1835, the Stow-on-the-Wold police were instrumental in the following convictions; one executed for murder,(Jeffrey), one transported for life, one transported for 14 years, and one transported for 7 years, and others for various terms of imprisonment.

Home Secretary, with all the advantages or rank, local connection, and the active support of Whigs and Radicals, is rejected in Devonshire by the Conservative interest, the landowners and occupiers who bring forward a country gentleman, hitherto unknown on the political arena. Whither shall the baffled Minister resort? To Tavistock, formerly a borough in the nomination of his father, the Duke of Bedford, and still nearly, if not quite, as much under his control as before the Reform bill was passed? That would be too bare-faced. At length an arrangement is made at Stroud whence, Lt. Col. Fox, son of Lord Holland, lately elected on the retirement of Mr. Hyett, is content to retire to make room for his political friend. Thus Stroud sinks into a Whig nomination borough, the Conservatives in the borough are too few to resist, the Ultra-Liberals are in a minority or look to Lord John Russell as one of themselves. Mr. Ricardo, however, a Whig of the old school is indignant at the transfer of the seat from a Whig scion of the nobility to a Whig Minister and tenders his support to the Conservative party with a view to the future success of a candidate from that party. He, like Hyett, had probably retired from the representation of the borough in disgust.

May 16th, 1835

Received a letter from my son at Prinknash Park. On the evening of his arrival Lord John Russell and Col. Fox called at Howell's. The canvass of the former at Stroud was then going on with a certainty of success. My son represents him as a very mean looking bilious person. He has recently married the widow of Lord Ribblesdale.

June 4th 1835

Rode to Stow. As I was going my horse stumbled and I was thrown over his head on the hard road. Not finding myself seriously hurt I went forward. My hat which did not fall off appears to have saved my head. Great reason have I to be grateful to Providence for a merciful deliverance. I believe I must discontinue riding on my harness horse; he has for sometime past been weak on his fore legs, yet may still be very serviceable as a harness horse.

June 6th, 1835

A very sultry day; distant thunder.

Mr. Billingsley called to arrange with me the terms which Mr. Harrison should be engaged to serve the church at Upper Slaughter during our proposed excursion to the North. It was settled that he should receive two guineas each Sunday, that he should undertake weekly duty, especially the preparation of the candidates for Confirmation, occupying my study and a bedroom, being waited on by the cook and housemaid, and stable boy whom we left in the house and being supplied with milk and vegetables from our dairy and garden.

June 8th, 1835

A very brilliant hot day.

After a very early breakfast, left home for the Metropolis, and drove to Stow, where at 6 a.m. I ascended the roof of a branch coach, which makes Oxford at 10 o'clock in time to transfer such of its passengers as proceed to London, by the Blenheim coach. I engaged my place from Stow to London: the coach to Oxford is drawn by two horses but is well appointed: from Oxford the conveyance is by an excellent and long established four-horse coach. Travelled to London by the Wycombe road and reached the Coach Office in Oxford Street by four o'clock. Was much struck by the luxuriant crops of a new clover, the *Trifolium incarnatum,* near High Wycombe. This beautiful scarlet plant has long been cultivated for ornament in flower gardens; but in France is cultivated as a productive and nutritious grass.

July 11th, 1836

Delightful weather. After breakfast, and after transacting business as a Magistrate, left Upper Slaughter with Edward in the open carriage for Cheltenham. All the smart farmers and tradesmen's families on the road to a gipsy *fête champêtre* at Casey Compton. Edward left me at Sandywell to botanize in the adjacent woods, and return in the open carriage. At the Plough a colloquy with Sir John Guise, while I was taking luncheon. Proceeded to Gloucester by a Bristol coach. Called on Mrs. and Miss Davies in Wellington Parade. Pursued my journey by coach to Newnham, a very lingering conveyance: about 10 miles. Preparations for Gloucester races in the meadows. By Over Bridge, having Highnam on the right, now occupied by one Baker, a merchant at Gloucester, passed through a rich country, full of orchards: a great show of apples. At Minsterworth the road passes close by the Severn: then the river makes a long detour, and is not seen from the road till near Westbury, where the remains of an old mansion of the Colchesters, with formal gardens, canals, yew hedges, statue of Neptune etc. [1]

Fine reach of the Severn, the Vale of Gloucester bounded by hills and the clothing district in the distance on the left: on the right the elevated and wooded heights of the Forest of Dean: a rich and fertile track. Through Broadoak to Newnham, a dull small town on a hill above the Severn where is a ferry to cross to the opposite bank. Mr. Parsons, one of the editors of the Oxford edition of the Septuagint, the incumbent. Mr. Harrison, who officiated for me during my absence in Yorkshire last summer, occupying my house at Upper Slaughter, was Curate of Newnham. Here I was met by Mr. Bathurst's carriage, which took me to Lydney Park about seven miles of undulating country, a very beautiful drive. Skirted the Forest of Dean, passing through what is called 'The Purlieu', a grove of oaks, with all the accompaniment of fern, stacks of bark etc. To the right Hay-hill, the residence of Revd. Edward Jones, on a commanding elevation backed by the fine woods of the Forest.

I omitted to mention between Westbury and Newnham on the right the richly wooded valley in which lies Flaxley Abbey, the seat of Sir Thomas Crawley-Boevey, and near it the residence of my old friend and brother Magistrate, the Revd. Charles Crawley. Crossed more than one rail road by which is conveyed to the Severn the coal and iron, stone and timber, the rich produce of the adjacent forest.

To the left the Severn expands into a fine estuary. Three miles from Newnham is Blakeney, a village in a lovely basin formed by low wooded hills. The road passes over the undulating margin of the Forest, the view to the left being over extensive levels of meadow land stretching along the northern shore of the Severn: the country studded with detached farm houses, the cottages by the road side numerous, each with its productive garden, and no lack of orcharding.

Lydney a large village without pretensions to neatness, or in any way striking: about a mile further to the right Lydney Park, a spacious mansion, not of modern date, backed by fine foliage. Reached my friends at eight p.m. who had dined, but soon supplied my lack of dinner. Mr. and Mrs. Bathurst had no other guests than

* Now owned by the National Trust.

Charles Bragge Bathurst (Senior) died 4 March 1831

myself. We were not long before we engaged in discussing the now prominent point of interest to County Magistrates — who shall succeed the worthy Cunningham as Governor of the County Gaol.

Strolled in the garden contiguous to the mansion under the shade of noble Spanish Chestnut trees, enjoying the odour of orange trees in full blossom amid thickets of rhododendron, deciduous cedars, and other luxuriant and uncommon exotic trees. Conversation closed the evening. The drawing room in which we sat contains a stiff full length portrait by Sir Godfrey Kneller of the first Lord Bathurst. This and the room in which dinner was served are spacious and lofty apartments. In the drawing room there is also a good bust of Lord Sidmouth by Westmacott.

July 12th, 1836

Rain had fallen during the night, the air was cooled, and the weather very enjoyable. Rose early, wrote and read before breakfast, which meal I took *tête-à-tête* with Mrs. Bathurst: Bathurst, according to custom, rising late and not making his appearance till it was time for him to repair to Lydney to attend a Justice meeting, which was followed by a Forest Court, at which as Verderer he administers justice under a special Act of Parliament to the inhabitants of that district. The Magistrates who met him were Mr. Ormerod, the Historian of Cheshire who resides near Chepstow, Mr. Morgan the Incumbent of Tidenham and another.

While he was so engaged, I whiled away the time with desultory reading till I settled to the cursory perusal of two rather elaborate MSS. of the late Mr. Bragge Bathurst, the father of my friend, for many years Chairman of our Sessions, as often as his public duties as Minister of the Crown under the administrations of Lord Sidmouth, Percival and Lord Liverpool would permit, until the chair devolved on Dr. Cooke, who of late years assigned it to Bathurst, the son. The ex-Minister was a laborious, indefatigable man, a sound scholar bred up in the legal profession, and of a disposition closely to follow out any subject which engaged his attention. Hence he devoted great research and learning in investigating the history of certain Roman remains within the park at Lydney, being two camps occupying two summits of two precipitate hills about half a mile from his mansion. They command a very fine and extensive prospect of the estuary of the Severn, and appear to have been an important and permanent station. The smaller one is, probably, the one originally selected as an exploratory fort, the larger, covering a considerable area, is remarkable for the remains of antiquity discovered there, partially known to exist throughout the 18th century, early in which the Bathurst family acquired this property, coins and pottery etc. being occasionally found, but closely investigated by excavations under the directions of the late Mr. B.

The result of his enquiries is that, in process of time and towards the close of the Roman sway in Britain, this camp had been converted into the residence of the *pro-prator* or other chief officer in command of the district; the excavations having disclosed the details of three separate and considerable edifices, one of which was clearly a villa, with numerous apartments, remains of tesselated pavements etc.; a second, a detached edifice containing a set of baths; and the third a temple. There is also the remains of a large tank or cistern for holding water, though it has not yet been ascertained from what spring, or by what channels the water was conducted thither. No notice of this station is contained in any of the itineraries. The particulars and reasoning on the subject are developed in the MSS to which I refer, and in an elaborate set of plans and drawings prepared under the late Mr. B's directions. Besides, there is a very large collection of antiquities found during the excavations, or collected at previous periods. These are very numerous and various — a vast collection of coins from Augustus to Constantius — pottery-iron implements of war, for domestic purposes, or handicrafts — ornaments of dress, rings, clasps, pins, combs, necklaces, spoons, chains, horse furniture and the like; with some votive inscriptions, bronze figures of dogs, a small bronze bust of the local deity, curious tessera understood to be used as stamps to be affixed to vessels containing medicaments, and metal letters used in inscriptions.

The remains of the temple afforded most scope to Mr. B's ingenious reasoning and research in which he availed himself of the works of eminent antiquaries, with references to Roman writers, and modern explorers of ancient remains ... The miniature bronze bust found in the remains close by resembles recognized busts and medallions of Asculapius, and the very frequent recurrence of figures of dogs among the articles found on the site of the temple leads to the conclusion that the healing Deity was the object of worship, it being recognized that, probably from a circumstance attached to the infant years of the God, as set forth in the old legends respecting him, dogs were considered sacred to him. One of these figures is a small bronze representation of a greyhound, of very tasteful and spirited workmanship: the others are more or less rude and homely.

Various indications seem to show that the villa and its accompanying edifices were destroyed by fire, and the site being from that time neglected and overgrown by timber, it was not till about a century ago that any attention was drawn to the antiquities on the spot. The eminence is known by the country people by the name of the Dwarf's Hill, and a persuasion still prevails that the fosses and buildings were the product of the labours of the diminutive fairy race.

Bathurst being detained longer than he expected at Lydney I set out with his very pleasing, accomplished and intelligent lady on a walk into the park: he met us on his return home, having come to seek us, and I prolonged my ramble with him till a late dinner hour. The house, a large rambling mansion first built in the close of the 17th century and frequently altered since, stands in the plain extending from the rising ground of the Park towards the Severn distant nearly a mile and half. The flower garden and shrubbery adjoin the principal apartments, are beautifully laid out, and rich in fine trees, especially the Spanish Chestnuts of very large growth and now in fine foliage and blossom. lFrom the drest grounds we entered the park which, though not comprising more than 200 acres, seems from the varied, undulating and in places steep and rocky ground, to occupy a much larger space. The camps are the leading features, being flanked by two deep and narrow glens, thro' each of which a small brook descends. The fern, the groups of deer, the fine timber and foliage combine in rendering the place very enjoyable, many paths with rude seats and a drive render the park accessible in various directions. Besides the noble chestnuts, oak, stately ash trees, gigantic thorns and yew trees, the indigenous lime, and maple abound, affording fine studies to the landscape painter, and enjoyment to the lover of scenery.

The lights and shadows were peculiarly beautiful today. The camps present grand views of the estuary of the Severn, and on the opposite bank we noticed Berkeley Castle, Thornbury, Alveston, Knoll, Aust Cliff, and more remote, Dundry Hill in Somersetshire. It was delightful to saunter with Bathurst amid his groves while he pointed to some picturesque group of trees, and mingled conversation on county business, men and matters with classical illusions and references, lightly touching on graver points, and passing from one topic to another with the talent of a vigorous mind improved by extensive reading and intercourse with various countries and a large circle of connexions and acquaintances. No stranger interrupted the lively unrestrained and confidential conversation of the evening, during which we at times reverted to several points of interest to us both in the arrangement of the public business of the county. Mrs. B. takes a lively part in all subjects which occupy her husband's attention.

July 13th 1836

A dull cloudy day, with brief gleams of sunshine, sometimes hazy, rain expected but did not fall till sometime after sunset. After breakfast wrote to my wife, took a stroll in the park, looked over Coleridge's Table Talk, conversed with Mrs. B. till nearly the hour for luncheon, when Charles Crawley arrived on a visit, and Bathurst made his appearance. Mr. Morgan and his daughter from Tidenham made a morning visit. When they had gone, B., Crawley and myself set out for a long walk. Leaving the park to the left we ascended a hill, and from its summit commanded an extensive prospect over the estuary of the Severn. Lingered on this eminence, following the track of an ancient excavation of the surface formed by iron miners in days of yore.

When conducted through rocky ground to a considerable depth these excavations which often occur in this district are locally called *scowls*. In the line of this deep and winding trench, and on its sides, grew a profusion of very aged, huge knotted and gnarled yews, each a study for an artist : the reticulation of the old roots as they sought the kindred soil, twining themselves over the fragments of rock, themselves almost as hard as the stone, was an interesting exhibition of the peculiar character of the species. One tree, B. said, measured in girth 21 feet.

From this summit Severn-ward the view was very extensive, and inland we caught the distant wooded heights and undulations of Dean Forest. Our walk led entirely through B's property, which in this direction is richly wooded — a little forest of his own, bordered by corn and pasture fields, separated by natural clumps of oak trees, here called *roughets.* Passing through one or more copses we entered a large woodland tract, the Tufts, bordering the Forest of Dean: the scenery here is very delightful, sheep browsing under the shade of the wood, the luxuriant growth of fern, the glades, the paths, through the wood, along which the charcoal burners were driving long strings of Galloways, mules and donkeys, each laden with its sack, and toiling onwards to some neighbouring forge — all these objects arrested my attention, while admiring the various foliage and elegant ramification of the tall umbrageous oaks, the tremulous birch, the gloomy yews, and the glossy holly trees.

From time to time we paused to view the line of the Dean

Forest's wooded heights, with a recently erected church perched on a hill alone, yet so situated as to form a central point to a considerable population of miners, whose cottages occupy the low valleys along which railroads convey the iron ore and coal to the little port of Lydney. Pools of water abound in this district, and some of these of large extent, artificially held up, serve to drive the wheels of three or four forges in a deep wooded valley along which we now returned.

Iron is here manufactured into plates, which are afterwards coated with tin at some works, not distant from the village of Lydney: all these works are held under Bathurst, and are driven not only by the power of water but also of steam. From the Forge Valley we crossed a hill by winding footpaths which led to the little town of Lydney, and thence homeward where several guests were to assemble at my friend's hospitable board. The party, besides Crawley and myself, consisted of the incumbent of Lydney, Mr. Morgan, a Canon of Hereford Cathedral with two very pleasing daughters, Mr. Bryan, Incumbent of Woollaston, Alvington and Peeston, and a young lady who remained to sleep at the mansion, whose name I did not catch. Agreeable and lively conversation, in which the varied information, quiet humour, and playfulness of B. shone forth, but not to greater advantage than the easy kindliness and simple manners of Mrs. B. whiled away the hours till midnight sent us to our repose.

July 14th, 1836

A very enjoyable day. The air bright and clear, and stirring, the sun occasionally shining brightly: clouds broken and high. Conversation with Crawley before breakfast: the nameless young lady of yesterday evening proved to be Mr. Bryan's daughter, and she left Lydney Park in the Bathurst's open carriage shortly after breakfast. Passed the forenoon in conversation with Crawley and Mrs. B. very pleasantly. B., as usual, not appearing till nearly the luncheon hour and at post time, when I received a joint letter from my wife and Edward.

An excursion into the Forest was planned: at first it was proposed that all should go in B's pony chaise, and Crawley's shandry-dan, but the former broke down on its return from conveyancing Miss Bryan to Woolaston, so the matter ended in the three gentlemen going in Crawley's carriage with a servant on horseback to open the gates.

The early part of the drive was in the same line as the

commencement of our walk yesterday: ascending the summit we pursued our course through a luxuriant copse or wood, and then came into a road leading to the left in a direction from Lydney to Bream, carried along the ridge of a hill, clothed more or less as all these summits are with oak coppice, interspersed with corn and pasture fields, and commanding fine views of the wooded heights and rich valleys of the Forest. Passed through Bream, a little hamlet with a small chapel, not of recent erection, and there struck into a Turnpike road leading to Coleford, soon entered Dean Forest properly so called, having before us that valley in which lies the Parkend collieries and iron forges — the view very fine — undulating eminences of fine outline, one sweeping behind another, chiefly crowned with noble oak woods — sequestered valleys of tangled copse, amidst which the birch and nut trees abounded — here and there a bare and turfy hillside, with miners' cottages approachable by winding tracks and paths: the common over which we passed planted with young oaks of a few years' growth, though unprotected by a fence, such being the system adopted by Mr. Machen of Whitemead Park, the Deputy Surveyor under the Crown, to keep up the supply of young timber.

On a wooded slope, and to our right, the modern church dedicated to St. Paul[1], which had been pointed out to me yesterday, with its adjacent parsonage and school house. Mr. Poole is the incumbent: in the valley beneath embowered in trees the residence of Mr. Machen in a lovely valley, somewhat marred by the dingy and huge iron forges, with their steam engines, smoke curling upwards through the foliage of the overhanging forest.

We approached Mr. M's sequestered and tasteful home by an excellent carriage road through one of the reserved walks which to the extent of 7000 acres, about one half of the Forest, have of late years been enclosed for the purpose of nourishing a supply of timber for the use of the naval department of government. Keys, furnished by the forest authorities to the neighbouring gentry, admit them into these verdant enclosures. At Whitemead Mr. Machen being from home at the time when we called, we left our carriage and horses and took a delightful walk for two hours through the dense forest forming the background of the Park end forges and coalpits. Here we were in the centre of a busy, swarthy population, now in full employ, the coal and iron trade being very flourishing; what were the wages of the adult I did not hear, but of

---

1 Parkend church designed by Rev. Henry Poole, 1822.

two brothers whom we questioned, boys of 15 or 16 and 10 or 12 years old, we ascertained that the elder earned nine and the younger three shillings weekly, with constant work. Yet are not these foresters quite easy: they are a secluded, ignorant, but manly and good humoured race, suspicious as to the purposes and probable results of recent enquiries made by a government commission of which Bathurst was a leading member, and which have led to many new regulations and plans which the free-miners consider to be infringements on their old forest laws and privileges, which they highly value, and greatly exaggerate.

Forgetful that their interests are best consulted by the speculations of foreigners, as they are called, opulent capitalists, who work the great mines, and so supply a regular occupation to the labouring chap with adequate wages. They are capable also of carrying on works requiring a far greater outlay in machinery, with a facility of more extensive mining operations than the united efforts of the free-miners could furnish. The latter sign for the antiquated rights which entitled them in petty companies to open mines, and search for ore and coal. Hence the origin of riots which disturbed this district a few years ago, and which it required the presence of the military to suppress : but not only are they uneasy in respect of their mining privileges, they conceive themselves ill used and injured by the enclosures formed by the government, and the steps taken to abate encroachments commonly made through-out the forest.

These wayward feelings are maintained by local agitators, law attorneys and the like, and in some instances fostered from without by parties actuated by electioneering motives. Pity it is that discontent should be thus encouraged, and ill will engendered among a simple, secluded people, who enjoy real and peculiar advantages in a regular demand for their labour, and the absence of all local taxation, the Dean Forest being wholly extra-parochial.

The principal forge which we passed in a gigantic grim mass of buildings, intersected by railway trucks, abounding in steam engines, frowning like some old timeworn fortress, whose huge, dingy battlements resound with the clang of ponderous hammers, the blast of giant bellows, and similar impressive noises, now louder, now more suppressed, as the varied operations proceed.

Higher up the hill we visited the mouth of one of the deepest and largest mines of the district, where the coal is raised from a pit nearly 200 yards below the surface. The works belong to Mr. Protheroe, who has an extensive concern in this district: we watched the ascent and descent of the tram carts, as they were lowered to the bottom of the pit, or raised by steam with a heavy load of coal. From a workman near the pit's mouth, a finely bronzed fellow with intelligent and handsome features, a bright eye, curly hair and form indicative of great bodily strength, we learnt that the persons employed below including boys, amounted to 100, and that eight horses were used at the bottom of the mine who, once admitted, never saw daylight again till age or accident incapacitated them for work.

The bed of coal is worked by partners; two generally contract for raising a certain portion of coal : these employing under them four or five more men and boys called *butties,* and each party knowing the exact limits of their working, disputes scarcely, if ever, arise between the operatives thus engaged.

Beyond this mine the forest spreads over undulating ground in a vast depth of shade; of underwood there is little, except on the margin of the streams which trickle down the hollows; but the oak trees are of noble girth and growth. We wandered amid their maze in various directions for an hour or more, admiring the fitful changes of light and shade, and the imposing grandeur and loneliness of the woodland scene, emerging from the wood nearly where we had entered it, and thence repairing to Mr. Machen's house, where we had left the carriage. I had known him before by meeting him as a Magistrate. M's drawing room exhibited a symptom of his late trip to Italy, in a very elegant alabaster model of the Falling Tower of Pisa.

Time would not allow us to linger long at Whitemead : we retraced our steps to Bream, and shortly after deviated into one of Bathurst's many woods to visit the so called Scowls, and truly curious and picturesque they are. Of primeval date, perchance relics of Roman miners, these excavations are of some hundred yards extent, in an irregular line, forming as far as we traced them a circle of unequal depth. The workmen of course followed the veins of iron ore, wherever they led them through the rocks: in places the narrow excavation is carried between masses of rock varying from 20 to 30 or 40 feet in height, curiously rifted masses, now perpendicular, and again overhanging or even leaning at the top against each other.

Through a bed of decaying leaves, over a rugged rocky bottom, we walked from one picturesque sort of grotto to another, often climbing from ledge to ledge. The whole is in the bosom of an extensive wood, and the summit of each mass of rock is more or less tufted with lofty timber trees, ash, oak, birch, yew or beech or lime, of which it is difficult to predicate what part is stem and what part root, for the latter seeking the soil has entwined itself down the surface, or within the crevices of the rock, swelling into thick limbs — hence partly acting as wedges, and partly affording a channel for rain. The lapse of years produces dislocation of the beds of rock, and a fall ensues, by which the rocks are tossed in wild confusion, new avenues are formed, new cavities are disclosed, while the trees themselves loosened from their hold fall into the excavation, blocking up the passage until removed. Nothing can be more striking than this sylvan scene: rugged in some parts, and boasting grace and elegance in others, where the ivy hangs in festoons, or a tuft or tall grass, or a trailing bramble hangs pensile over the face of rock.

We amused ourselves with imagining the tenants of the adjacent Roman Camps, or villa, superintending the mining operations carried on for the public profit by the sturdy and subdued natives of the district. Our homeward route led through a narrow waggon track traversing the wood, thickly overgrown, and not very penetrable except by as steady an animal as the one which drew Crawley's shandry-dan.

A late dinner, with an evening of varied conversation, partly on antiquities, partly on domestic architecture, general literature, and anecdote not unmingled with discussion on county matters, brought to a close a most agreeable day.

July 15th, 1836
When I rose the rain was falling in soft fertilizing showers. The forenoon continued very soaking, and our friends strove most kindly to persuade Crawley and myself to forego our design of leaving them. Bathurst appeared soon after 12 o'clock, and soon after arrived from Pencraig near Ross, a Mr. H. Clifford, a Herefordshire gentleman, and one of B's colleagues as a Commissioner of the Forest of Dean. Having lingered later than we had proposed, and I having held a parting conference with B. on county matters, about 2 o'clock Crawley and myself took leave of our excellent and friendly host and hostess, with every probability of pouring rain on our way to Newnham, to which place Crawley kindley conveyed me in his open carriage. But we had hardly passed the village of Lydney when the sky cleared, the sun appeared, and the weather was delightful.

At four o'clock I reached Newnham, hired a gig, and by a little after five, was set down at the Bell at Gloucester. Finding that not any conveyance by coach to Cheltenham could be had for an hour, and being anxious to reach home before it was dark, I proceeded without delay in a chariot from the Bull which Mr. Marsh agreed to my taking at the same price as a fly. By 6 o'clock I reached the Plough Hotel, and found a letter from my wife brought by Bowles, who was waiting and with my phaeton and horse. Now fell a heavy storm of rain, threatening a wet evening: after taking some slight refreshment I set out for Upper Slaughter in the wet, which however ceased before I passed Charlton, and the close of my journey was dry, though cold. Before nine I rejoined my family; all pretty well. I had much to tell, and somewhat to hear, which occupied us till bedtime.

July 16th, 1836

Rain had fallen during the night, but the day was fine, a brisk air stirring and towards evening it was cool. Wrote to F. Aston to thank him for a letter which arrived during my absence at Lydney Park, in which was mentioned Lord and Lady Wemyss's expected arrival at Stanway. As yesterday or today was named, with a suggestion that if we made a visit to his Lordship concur with one to Lady Lyttelton we should make the Vicarage at Wood Stanway a baiting place, as we went and returned. Told him our design of going to Malvern on Monday, when Edward and myself would be glad to act upon his kind suggestion, both going and returning.

After breakfast engaged with Pearce in examining the draft minutes of the transactions of the Board of Guardians on Thursday last, making an abstract of them and considering various points as to the working of the Stow Union, especially as to the purchase of land for a workhouse.

July 18th, 1836

A fine day with a clear air, cool and somewhat windy. After breakfast accompanied by Edward, set out for Peach Field Lodge on a visit to my aunt, Lady Lyttelton, in my open carriage with our servant. At Stanway paid our respects to Lord and Lady Wemyss, who arrived there on Saturday with two of the Lady Charterises. His Lordship was lying on a sofa, suffering severely from spasm, and looking very ill and emaciated. Lady W. apparently in her usual good health. After a short visit, walked to the Vicarage where the Astons expected us, with whom we took luncheon. I sent for George Cook, and settled with him the Lady-day rent. About three o'clock continued our journey by Twyning Fleet to Stratford

Bridge Inn, where we baited our horse for an hour, and arrived at Peach Field Lodge by seven o'clock. Found Lady L. looking extremely well, and in good spirits.

Passing through the parish of Bredon, as we approached Twyning Fleet, we noticed mistletoe growing on several Black Italian Poplars, a very unusual habitat, as we conceived: but from a paper in "The Analyst" which I happened to notice it appears to be not uncommon. It is there stated that the mistletoe is wont to grow only on one species of a genus, for instance, on the Black Poplar, and not on the Abele, aspen etc. — on the apple, and not on the pear tree; Ray, however, speaks of the mistletoe growing on the pear tree.[1]

July 26th, 1836

With Edward left home in our open carriage for Stanway where we were very kindly received by Lord Wemyss. Lady Wemyss' party consisted of herself, her two daughters, Lady Grey of Groby and Lady Jane Charteris, Col. Wildman and a sweet girl of ten years old, daughter of Lady Grey, who is a young widow in mourning for her husband, the eldest son of the Earl of Stamford. She is a very pleasing person, and would have been handsome had she not lost her left eye by an accident many years since. Col. Wildman as the widower of Lady Margaret C. is very much domesticated with the Wemyss family, a gentleman-like and pleasing man. Lord W. joined our dinner party and enjoyed the society of his family circle, mingling in conversation very freely, rather deaf, extremely thin, and somewhat infirm but capable of more exertion than one would at first sight expect. He appears highly pleased with the state of his Gloucestershire property, and the management of his steward, Mr. C. Marshall and takes great interest in his plantations, in the luxuriant growth of the timber, and in planning improvements and repairs.

August 3rd, 1836

A fine and warm day. As soon after breakfast as I had dismissed a pertinacious woman, the wife of a publican at Stow, who had been fined last week by the Magistrate and solicited my

---

1 The race of mistletoe in Great Britain will grow on any broad-leafed tree or shrub; but is very rare on oak.

intervention to get the fine reduced I left home in the phaeton for Stanway to officiate at the funeral of poor old Aston. Arrived at the Vicarage soon after 12 where I found the two sons from London. Soon after 1 the procession left Wood Stanway, a mourning coach preceding the hearse and another following it. The body was deposited in a stone vault near the wall of the church on the north side, adjacent to the Vicar's pew. I parted with the family at the entrance to the church yard and having thus performed the last duties to an aged, respected and worthy friend returned home to receive a party at dinner. We entertained the Dean of Gloucester, with his son Henry and his daughters, Cecil and Louisa, Captain Leigh, Mr. George Daubeny, and Mrs. Wynniatt, and her son and daughters.

August 6th, 1836

Dined earlier than usual in anticipation of Sophia Hunt's departure, as we proposed, for Gloucester by the Novelty coach. We all walked with her to Eyford where we arrived some time earlier than the coach usually passes : but it had already passed several minutes before. Edward promptly ran back to fetch our phaeton. The servants with the luggage conveyed it to the gate leading from Upper Slaughter into the Cheltenham road: thither I accompanied Sophia. In a short time Edward brought our carriage and conveyed our friend to Naunton Inn, where she took a fly and proceeded to Cheltenham, in the expectation of reaching Gloucester tonight.

August 8th, 1836

Busy with workmen, mason, slater and carpenter, who began to-day to take off the slate of the chancel, which needs to be repaired.

August 10th, 1836

Very fine weather. Breakfasted early and soon after 7 left home in the open carriage for Cheltenham on my way to attend an adjourned Quarter Session at Gloucester for the appointment of a Gaoler in the room of poor Cunningham. Found a coach ready to start and reached Gloucester by half past 10. To the Bell Hotel where I met a large party of Conservative Magistrates many of whom had attended the annual meeting and dinner of the Blue

Club yesterday. The party assembled to the number of nearly 130 and the reports made as to the strength of the Conservative interests in both divisions of the County were stated to me to have been very satisfactory.

As this was the Commission day of the Summer Assizes most of the Magistrates remained in Gloucester to be ready for the opening of the Court on the following day, and these were the Lord Lieutenant (Segrave), the four County members, Lords Edward and Granville Somerset, Bathurst, etc. If so many magistrates had not been assembled the High Sheriff, Gist, would have had a meagre attendance at his dinner, being a person but little known in the County, as it was more than forty dined with him at the Bell Hotel at 7 o'clock of whom I was one. The Judges Littledale and Patterson had arrived at about 6 o'clock. Gist was attended by Archdeacon Timbrill as his Chaplain and acquitted himself creditably in the Chair.

One of the persons, whose appearance excited most remark was Grantley Berkeley, who seemed to brave the comments likely to be made upon his recent exploit in violently assaulting in London, Frazer, the editor of a noted Conservative magazine in which our honourable member's recently published novel, *Berkeley Castle,* had been severely criticized. It is not possible to justify the spirit of the critique, which besides censuring with apparent justice the work, as remarkable for loose principle, silly writing, anachronism and the like, made the history and private character of the present generation of the Berkeleys and their immediate progenitors, the matter of most harsh and stringent comment. Lord Segrave, his mother, his father, the author of the book, and the scandalous record of the house, were all exhibited in a tone of bitter and trenchant satire.

Frazer was, therefore, assailed with brutal violence in his own shop: on hesitating to name the author of the article, was cruelly horsewhipped by Grantley Berkeley while his brother Craven stood at the door to prevent any person entering to protect the object of the irritated author's wrath. In this the younger brothers only followed the example given by the senior, Lord Segrave, on a somewhat similar occasion in Cheltenham several years ago, when the Editor of the County newspaper was treated with like ferocity by the peer, then Col. Berkeley, enraged by the insertion of an article severely commenting on the notorious irregularities of his conduct.

Frazer appeared before the London Magistrate covered with wounds and bruises: the magistrate warmly censured the perpetrators of the assault: the brothers affected to glory in their shame: the magistrate doubted about admitting them to bail: the assailants rather lowered their tone and gave assurance that they would abstain from further threat and violence: bail to a heavy amount was accepted: and Grantley and Craven Berkeley will be tried for the assault. But the matter did not rest here. Dr. Maginn an Irish physician, formerly an army surgeon, and Editor of *the Standard* called at Berkeley House to avow himself the author of the offensive article in the magazine, and a duel ensued. Three shots were fired by each combatant, but neither were wounded and the parties left the ground.

Miserable is the state of society which prevails that such proceedings should be considered consistent with honour, and that the man (Grantley Berkeley) should post away from such scenes and doings to sit as a Magistrate on the bench of this county and as a Grand Juror to hold an inquest on persons charged with crimes many of a far lighter grade than those which he had committed!

Before retiring to my lodging I walked for half an hour with Bathurst and coversed with him on the occurrences of the day, and points connected with magisterial duty.

August 11th, 1836

A very lovely summer's day.

Breakfasted with a party of Conservative Magistrates at the Bell Hotel …. attended Divine Service at the Cathedral where the Archdeacon of Gloucester preached a long and very commonplace sermon before the Judges of Assize: his text — be quiet and study to do your own business – exhorting men to personal reformation, loyalty, obedience, submission to the laws, and the like. Attended in the Crown Court …

I retired before the first trial was concluded and putting myself into a fly arrived by 5 o'clock at the house of my excellent friends the Howells. The young man from Upper Slaughter had reached Prinknash Park on horseback half an hour before me, and brought a good account of his mother and grandmother. Much conversation and cheerful enjoyment of the family circle filled up the evening agreeably.

August 12th, 1836

A very fine summer's day. Between breakfast and dinner whiled away the time with Howell in walking through Pope's Wood and over Painswick Hill to call on Hyett[1] whom we found at home suffering from gout in his hand but otherwise well and in good spirits ... politics, literature, poor laws, railways, lunatic asylums and other topics formed the miscellaneous matter of our conversations both at Hyett's house and as he accompanied us homewards as far as Painswick Beacon on the summit of which we lingered enjoying the coolness of the breeze and the splendid prospect which the eminence afforded.

Mr. Hyett's house and grounds very enjoyable, especially his library and dining room.[2] In the latter he has lately introduced, as a border to the floor, some beautiful parquetring in various patterns, lozenges, etc. each separate piece being formed of highly polished specimens of various woods, chiefly of English species.

We returned only in time to dress for dinner and to our home party were added Mr. Wintle of Saintbridge House and his nephew T. Fulljames, the architect and County Surveyor.

August 13th, 1836

Left Prinknash at one o'clock with Howell by the Bath coach for Cheltenham where my open carriage met us. Arrived at Upper Slaughter between 5 and 6 o'clock. Edward and I assisted Howell in folding up and directing a large packet of circulars for manufacturers in this section of the Inspector's district to be dispatched by post to-morrow. It appears that the Government requires the Inspectors to enforce the provisions of the Factory Act with increased energy and more minute supervision.

August 17th, 1836

Lovely weather, bright and warm with a stirring breeze on the hills. After breakfast set out with my wife and Howell in the Phaeton on a Factory circuit. Our first point Blockley which is a most enjoyable village situate in a deep valley accessible on most sides only by steep hills embowered in woods.

The village itself is built on undulating ground with a handsome ancient church in the centre, standing on a knoll in a cemetery

---

1   W.H. Hyett, the former M.P.
2   Wings, etc. were added to the house in the 1830s by George Basevi, the architect brother-in-law of Hyett. The grounds are recorded in Thomas Robins's picture of 1748 for Benjamin Hyett, full of rococo follies.

containing some fine elm trees. We did not enter the church but
through an open window I could see that it was spacious and
handsome with several monuments to the Rushout — Lord
Northwick — family. Adjacent to the church the comfortable ivy
clad parsonage, and near it another ivy clad residence of one of the
silk throwsters of the place ... and there are other comfortable and
respectable dwellings, some antique, others modern evidently
occupied by persons in easy circumstances: the whole being built of
the excellent freestone of the parish or from the adjoining quarries
on Bourton Hill. There is an air of prosperity about the place, a
new Dissenting Meeting House, etc.

Howell inspected the six silk mills. These are all on a small scale,
ancient establishments but in full activity. We accompanied him to
two of these under the management of Messrs. Smith and Banbury.
The residence and garden of the latter gentleman are very pretty. It
is but a small stream by which these mills are worked. The produce
of the labour is sold at Coventry chiefly; some of it is consumed in
London. Bengal and Turkey silk are here manufactured into silk
thread. The process seems simple and the operatives chiefly young
females and boys from 8 to 10 years of age. They are not limited by
the Factory Act in respect of age but only as to the hours of
working, as regards young persons under 18. The new regulations
as to keeping registers of the hours of working, in three different
forms, recently required by the Board of Trade and now in the
course of being enforced by the inspectors, are applicable to these
silk mills. Howell was engaged in explaining these forms to the
different masters for nearly two hours. There is a strong Dissenting
interest in the place, nearly all the silk throwsters being seceders
from the church.

About 2 o'clock we proceeded to Campden, three miles distant
by a very rough and hilly road, during the greater part of which we
skirted   Northwick Park. The views are extensive over a fine
undulating country and the tower of Campden church a noble
object in the prospect. At Campden we baited our horse at the
principal Inn, a very clean and neat place and while Howell was
visiting the only silk mill propelled by water power, we visited the
splendid church. The inspector found here symptoms of prosperity
in trade. The Mill owner is about to erect a steam engine of 12 horse
power; and a new mill has been established in which the works are
propelled by two horses: this mill, however, being driven by animal
power, does not come under the provisions of the Factory Act.

Campden is a dull, clean, disused market town. In former times
of greater prosperity it was the seat of an active trade in woollen

cloths: but those days and that trade have long since passed away; the only remaining indications are the ancient market house situate in the fine wide street, with many good houses of a century or more in standing and others boasting a much higher antiquity with gable ends, fine oriel windows and other remains of the domestic architecture of by-gone centuries.

The church itself lofty, spacious, and of fine recent Gothic architecture contains a splendid assemblage of marble monuments and sculpture in a chapel where rest the remains of the distinguished families of Hicks and Noel. I enjoyed revisiting and showing them to my wife. Of late years ... the church has been newly pewed, ceiled and heated with warm water, the comfort of the congregation being greatly increased, with some deviations from a correct taste, particularly as regards the incongruous ornaments on the ceiling. We returned home and arrived at Upper Slaughter about 6 p.m. having enjoyed our little excursion much.

September 6th, 1836

After breakfast rode to Upper Guiting to attend the sale of the celebrated Southdown flock of the late Mr. Talbot. The high estimation in which Talbot was held as an agriculturalist and the great attention he had paid to the breed of his Southdowns, and Devonshire horned cattle, attracted a large assembly of people not only from the county but also from distant parts. The arrangements were very judicious and the sheep which were of exquisite symmetry and for the most part in excellent condition, were sold at high prices. Baker[1] laid out more than £100.

September 12th, 1836

At half-past two left Cheltenham by a Bristol Coach which set me down by half-past four at the lodge leading to Hardwicke Court, whence I walked to the house situate in a flat meadow with a few fine trees. The house[2], spacious, modern and comfortable in the Villa style, commands a fine view of the hills above Haresfield, Standish etc. The gentlemen of the party were shooting, the ladies walking so that I sat in an enjoyable library alone till Baker[3]

1 T.J. Lloyd Baker.
2 Built in 1818 by Sir Robert Smirke for T.J. Lloyd-Baker.
3 T.J. Lloyd-Baker.

arrived; the rest gradually dropt in, and at half past six all were assembled for dinner. Good cheer and lively conversation. The library and dining room contain some good family portraits: an excellent resemblance of my old acquaintance, now deceased, the Rev. Mr. Baker of Stout's Hill,[1] father of my host.

September 13th, 1836

A fine autumnal day. Strolled in the grounds before breakfast. The situation of Hardwicke Court does not admit of much variety in the disposition of the ornamental appendages of a mansion. Being quite flat and without pure water, all that could be done was to plant shrubberies, intersected by walks leading to greenhouse, aviary, root house, flower gardens, rockery and the like. Much pains have been taken to contrive a sequestered hermitage by an old moat,[2] once the limit of the formal gardens attached to the ancient mansion for which Baker has substituted his present comfortable abode. The water, indeed is muddy and its banks clayey: nature denied rocks but money has brought huge stones singular from their form and fossil remains, among which grow the usual assortment of rock plants such as ladies love to collect around their favoured nooks of taste and retirement.

At a late hour breakfast was ready. At 12 o'clock the party separated, Phelps betook himself to Chavenage, his residence near Tetbury, Barwick Baker to Gloucester and thence to visit Lord Edward Somerset at Ampney near Cirencester, his conveyance a Phaeton with fly away steads, old Baker and myself in a humble gig wended our way to Gloucester where we arrived as the Magistrates were congregating for the election of a Governor of the Gaol. We assembled in the Crown Court, Bathurst presiding. One hundred and six justices were assembled. The Lord Lieutenant Lord Segrave, the Duke of Beaufort, Lord E. Somerset, Lord Bathurst, Lord Redesdale were present, and most of the leading gentry both Conservative and Whigs, but there was a large preponderence of the latter actuated by a double motive, to bring in a partizan and shew the strength of the party on the one hand and on the other to favour a man to whom on the score of poverty the appointment

1 Stout's Hill, Uley, was built in Gothic style in 1743 by William Halfpenny for a clothier called Gyde. It was later bought by the Bakers before they settled at Hardwicke. It is now a preparatory school where Captain Mark Phillips was educated.
2 The remains of a canal in the Dutch manner.

Thomas John Lloyd-Baker of Hardwicke Court

was of the utmost importance and who was connected with some old and influential families.

September 13, 1836

I had been invited by Goodrich to meet the Bathursts at dinner at Matson and accompanied them in their carriage. Mrs. Goodrich and two daughters were absent in Devonshire for sea bathing. The two younger Goodrichs who are in the Army did not dine with us, having an engagement in Gloucester at the theatre at a representation of *The Hunchback*, a popular play by Sheridan Knowles. I strolled in the grounds about the house which Goodrich rents from Lord Sydney. It lies at the foot of the beautiful and finely timbered eminence Robins Wood Hill, is a truly Gloucester-shire old fashioned gable-ended mansion,[1] only so far modernized as to meet the habits of the present age in two very enjoyable drawing rooms with an oak-wainscotted dining room. The gardens remain nearly as in those days when a bowling green, sloping terraces, and canals were the acme of taste; but the ornamental timbers very fine, magnificent firs, oaks, larches, cedars, and Portugal laurels one of which is of enormous size and bulk exceeding the largest in my grounds at Upper Slaughter.

September 20th, 1836

A call from John Perkins, Junior, who had come from Oxford to Lower Swell accompanied by Mr. Underwood,[2] an architect, to select on the vicarage land a site for a parsonage which he proposes to begin building with funds obtained from Queen Anne's bounty, the Pincot Charity, the Dean and Chapter of Christchurch etc.

September 21st, 1836

Finished adapting a sermon from Bishop Horne on *the divine presence in holy places,* to be preached shortly in obedience to the King's letter recently transmitted to the clergy with a view to a collection in aid of the Incorporated Society for the enlargement and building of Churches.

1 King Charles I's headquarters during the Siege of Gloucester.
2 Henry Jones Underwood.

September 26th, 1836

Much engaged in the forenoon with the mason, carpenter and engineer in planning alterations and repairs to the foundation and part of the pewing of the church, and laying out the line for the pipes by which water is to be laid to my house.

April 1st, 1837

A frosty morning and a fine day. Alarmed soon after breakfast by the information that a fire had broken out in the village; a building used as an outhouse and close behind two cottages having caught fire in consequence of a careless young woman ... The hovel was thatched, with another thatched building adjoining, also faggot piles near. My son and myself with our men servants, and many labourers and others of the village were soon on the spot, and by copious supply of water from the brook in buckets soon arrested the further progress of the flames, the walls only of the hovel being left standing. The cottagers who used the building as outhouses lost some useful articles and tools.

I accompanied my son on a walk to Joiner's Down to look for the rare little plant *Thlaspi perfoliatum,*[1] which is coming into blossom. This species of Shepherd's Pouch, known to former English botanists as growing on the oolitic downs near Burford, has long escaped the discovery of modern seekers, till it was found by my son on my farm and adjacent stony banks about two years since. He has since met with it on other parts of the Cotswold hills, and furnished the Botanic garden at Oxford with specimens.

April 4th, 1837

My son had ridden to Sudeley to be present at the annual Cheltenham Steeple Chase, and returned to dinner. He reported the result; that an immense crowd of carriages, horsemen and pedestrians had been congregated, that fifteen horses started, of whom five were placed, the stakes being won by Capt. Lamb's Vivian. The winner of last year, Standard, then the property of W. Bryan of Lower Slaughter, now of V. Dolphin, and on both occasions ridden by W. Smith of Eyford, came in fifth. The Marquis of Waterford with his fine horse was distanced. It is the

---

1 Perfoliate penny-cress.

mania of the day thus to tempt Providence. The ground selected was in the valley stretching from Winchcombe towards Charlton Abbots, a course of five miles with the due proportion of fences, walls, hill, dale, brook and roads to cross, etc. The scene must have been very animated.

April 10th, 1837

A very hard frost and cold day with snow and sleet showers. After an early breakfast left home to attend the Easter Quarter Sessions at Gloucester. At the Bell joined Mr. Bathurst whom I found busy reducing into form the proposed code of prison regulations. Mrs. Bathurst was assisting him in copying his rough drafts; but she soon left for Lydney Park, and Bathurst remained with Purnell who had arrived from Stancombe Park and whom it is proposed to place on the committee of accounts. Bathurst looked in upon me at the Grand Jury Room, and went to transact some business at the Gaol, where I joined him after six o'clock. We dined together with Purnell at the Bell and the rest of the evening was occupied in auditing the accounts of the Bridewells, and in considering the Prison regulations. Retired to my lodgings a little before midnight.

April 24th, 1837

A beautiful spring day. Much alarmed about mid-day by a sudden fainting fit which deprived Mrs. Backhouse of all consciousness ... Dr. Hayward recommended some alteration of diet; but Mrs. B. is so particular in her dislike of many things which would be good for her, and in partiality to food unsuitable, that it is doubtful whether his advice will be closely followed.

May 13th, 1837

Rode to Stow, it being the second day of the Fair, where I transacted Justice business. Edward joined me from Oxford. He had started early in the morning with a friend for Barrington Inn in a gig, where they breakfasted. The forenoon was occupied in fishing in the Windrush; but owing to the cold showers with indifferent success.

May 29th, 1837

The King is believed to be suffering from asthma and water on the chest, and if the latter is not removed, a fortnight more may see a new reign. The heiress of the throne, the Princess Victoria of Kent, attained her eighteenth birthday on Wednesday last, and is capable of ascending the throne without a regency, as Queen in her own right.

June 11th, 1837

"A dripping June brings all in tune."

June 13th, 1837

Edward rode to Kingham to call on Mr. Curtis,*the naturalist,to whom he had been introduced at Oxford, and who is visiting Mr. Lockwood, and, being invited to dine and sleep there, sent Mr. L's servant for a change of dress.

June 14th, 1837

Edward returned from Kingham soon after 11 o'clock accompanying Mr. Lockwood and Mr. Curtis in the former's phaeton, L's servant riding Edward's horse. Mr. Curtis,[1] who is the proprietor of a splendid work, which has been in the process of publication for several years, illustrative of botany and entomology, the drawings for the plates being beautifully executed by himself, was attracted hither that he might visit the habitat of the rare *Thlaspi perfoliatum,* and other plants on the Rectory Farm, and at the same time form some notion of the entomological riches of the Cotswolds. Edward accompanied them to Bowman's hay and Joiner's downs, the naturalist and Mr. L. being provided with entomological gauze nets, and other apparatus, and catching some curious moths and beetles.

1 John Curtis, the entomologist, and artist, who contributed for several years to William Curtis's (no relation) Botanical Magazine, and wrote and illustrated *British Entomology* (16 vols.) 1824-39

June 15th, 1837

Very fine summer's day. Edward started on horseback at an early hour for Cirencester, whither he went in the expectation of finding a rare plant in Lord Bathurst's park, which he explored in vain under the guidance of the Misses Croome. He dined with Mr. Robert Croome and rode home by moonlight.

I proceeded to Stow to take evidence with the view to the committal of a prisoner charged with stealing two sovereigns and a half out of a poor blind man's box. The case had already been before me and Mr. Pole at my house on the 12th, when we had remanded the man for re-examination. After hearing the evidence of one witness, we were obliged by the pressure of other business to suspend the examination and sent him to the lock-up house about 12 o'clock. When about 5 in the afternoon the officer was sent to bring the prisoner before us, he was found dead, having strangled himself by forcibly tightening his neck cloth, a wretched example of living without God in the world, a wild, reckless, hardened life of idleness and vice.

June 20th, 1837

Received the melancholy news of the death of Mrs. Twisleton, the amiable wife of our neighbour, the Rector of Adlestrop. She had been confined of a seventh child, all living, about ten days ago. Her poor husband incautiously announced to her that their tenant and next door neighbour Bryan, had, in a paroxysm of grief, caused by his wife's death, attempted suicide. Poor Mrs. T. was so shocked, a nervous fever was induced which carried her off this morning. To Twisleton the loss is irreparable. He is but little versed in the ways of the world, is fanciful, absent, and has few practical views of things.

It is currently reported that the King departed this life yesterday at 5 p.m.

June 24th, 1837

A brilliant summer day. My son rode with me to Stow to attend the ceremony of proclaiming Queen Victoria. A subscription having been raised to fee the bell ringers and musicians, a humble procession was got up, headed by the Rector, myself and my son, the clerk proclaiming our Sovereign Lady in four stations, with "God Save the Queen" by the Band, cheers by the crowd, the inner circle being formed by the principal tradesmen. The proclamation over took luncheon at the Rectory with the Vavasour family.

June 26th, 1837

A very delightful day. At 8 o'clock left home for Gloucester to attend the Quarter Sessions. My wife accompanied me in the chariot to Cheltenham to purchase mourning (for the King). At the Shire Hall was occupied considering the evidence lately taken by the Sheriff, Trye, as to the charge made against the executioner of the murderer, Bartlett, sentenced at the last Assizes. It was alleged that he had been intoxicated and treated the corpse of the wretched sufferer with brutal levity and coarseness in view of the spectators. The account of such bad conduct had been mentioned in the House of Lords. A paragraph had been inserted in the Gloucester Journal by a Quaker, an inhabitant and tradesman of Gloucester, with a view to show that the punishment of death, as being generally insufficient to awe the minds of the spectators, might well be abolished, as barbarous and anti-Christian. Hence arose a controversy on the subject, the principal writer, a clever Quaker, Samuel Bowly,[1] denouncing the punishment of death.

July 8th, 1837

A very hot and brilliant day. Nearly finished hay making, a very fine crop, got up without a drop of rain. The funeral of his late Majesty is fixed for this evening.

July 10th, 1837

A very fine but hot day. Left home for Cirencester in my open carriage with my son. We passed an hour and a half in a call at Mr. Robert Croome's, where we saw his antique maiden sister, a *Venus*

---

1 Samuel Bowly was born in Cirencester in 1802. His father was in business as a cheese-factor in Cirencester and also a miller at Arlington Mill, Bibury. As a youth he was employed chiefly in the mill, and formed an evening school for the instruction of village boys. He later became a well-known philanthropist, a Temperance Reformer, was prominent in the anti-slavery agitation, and repeal of the Corn Laws. He lived at Saintbridge House, near Gloucester after the Wintles and before the Birchalls. Arlington Mill is now a museum, and Saintbridge House an Old People's Home.

barbata, and his brother-in-law Edward Daubeny, Rural Dean of Cirencester Deanery. Cirencester has been much improved of late years. The fine old church and the Town Hall, over the church porch which has been renovated, are now detached from mean and encroaching buildings which disfigured the market place, and have been removed by a judicious widening of the road, in effecting which Lord Bathurst showed much liberality.

At the coming election, two Conservative representatives for Cirencester are expected to be returned. Lord Edward Somerset retires from Parliament and Mr. Cripps will doubtless retain his seat. Lord Edward will probably be replaced by a young aspirant, the son of Colonel Master, of Knole Park, who is connected with the town as in course of time, on the decease of his relatives Miss Master and Lady John Thynne, the Abbey with its considerable estates, will devolve to Colonel Master.

July 11th, 1837

Walked with Margaret to make a morning call at Eyford. Not admitted, as Mrs. Dolphin was preparing to set off with Mr. D. to Gloucester to attend the races to-morrow. He is Steward.

July 12th, (Wednesday) 1837

A beautiful day. Wrote to the London Fishmonger to order fish for a dinner party on Friday.

July 15th, 1837

Rode with Edward to Stow: much conversation with him as to his future prospects, his going into the church, and settlement in life. All is tending towards what I anticipated when the connection with Miss Sketchley was abandoned by him. His partiality for Sophy Vavasour is maturing into a steady attachment. Except in respect of the lady's prospects as to fortune being scanty, we do not see any reason to oppose my son's wishes; she is not handsome, but she is sensible, amiable, well and prudently brought up, and the family connections very respectable ... Called on the Vavasours; saw all the family. Mr. V. walked with us on our way home as far as Lower Swell.

Sophy Vavasour at the time of her marriage

July 23rd, 1837

A very close sultry day with two or three heavy showers of rain. Read prayers and preached at Stanway in the forenoon: rode to Cutsdean and there read prayers and preached. Evening prayers at Stanway after which walked with Mrs.F.Aston and her children to Wood Stanway, where I passed half an hour, returning in time to meet the rest of the party who had been taking airings in different directions. Lady Wemyss in an open carriage driving Lady Belhaven, and the Ladies Charteris, accompanied by my son on horseback having visited the Gists at Wormington Grange, and Lords Wemyss and Belhaven having taken a ride; Lord W. very cheerful, interested in his Gloucestershire property, and taking a delight in Stanway. F. Aston having gone to Upper Slaughter yesterday evening returned to the Vicarage at Wood Stanway this evening.

July 25th, 1837

A letter from Mr. Cox the Conservative agent for the Eastern Division of the County, stating that an opposition to Mr. Codrington is threatened, and soliciting a subscription to a fund to secure his return. This looks very like as if the secret compact made in the county by leaders of the Conservative and Whig interests was about to be infringed. The Whig leader, Lord Segrave is putting forth his strength in the boroughs of Cheltenham, Gloucester and Bristol where the three brothers are opposed by Conservatives. It is a bold enterprise for the Berkeley family. His Lordship has a long purse, is ambitious, and anything but scrupulous. His brothers Craven Berkeley at Cheltenham and Frederick Berkeley at Gloucester, are active, acute, not burdened by high principle, and ready to possess even destructive opinions, so that they secure the mob.

August 4th, 1837

Reached Gloucester about 1 o'clock. On calling at the Palace found the Bishop engaged with other clergymen and sat for some time with Mrs. Monk. My object in seeking a conference with his Lordship was to obtain his promise to receive my son as a candidate for ordination at the Christmas ordination. The Bishop very cordially and kindly acceded to my request. Dined at the Bell, it being the anniversary dinner of the Governor of the Gloucester

Infirmary,which is always holden in the week of the Summer assizes under the stewardship of the High Sheriff [1] of the past year. On this occasion Mr. Gist presided, who sadly disgraced himself, having arrived at Gloucester in a state of high excitement and under the influence of morning potations. Although the party was not large and composed of steady gentlemen, he soon showed that the wine he was drinking had overpowered his little discretion so that at a later hour, after rambling in the street, and it is to be feared, exposing himself there, he became still more offensive, swearing and talking obscenely. Had a gentleman presided the party would have been very agreeable.

August 15th, 1837

Dined at the Wallers, Farmington Lodge, meeting the bride and bridegroom from Bourton-on-water (R. Waller and his wife), Mr. Talbot,[2] son of Lord Talbot, Rector of Withington, a very pleasing young man, Reginald Wynniatt with his sisters Kitty and Fanny, etc. A cheerful party and much conservative triumphing over the success of the party at the late County elections, not constrained by the presence of young Wynniatt of Whig-Liberal stock.

September 12th, 1837

Accompanied Margaret and my son in the chariot to Cheltenham where Edward was going to spend a day or two with Lady Arbuthnot, the friend whom Emily and Sophy Vavasour were visiting. Lady A. is a very pleasing person of middle age residing in an elegant house of her own in Montpellier Parade. She is the separated wife of an officer in the army, who married her for her fortune being greatly in debt. Lady A. found his embarrassments so serious as to make it highly unwise to liquidate them and they consequently parted. She allows him sufficient income to reside abroad, and herself has fixed her abode at Cheltenham. She is much attached to Sophy and was anxious to become acquainted with Edward. Met Howell and his son Frederick. They were

---

1 Samuel Gist of Wormington Grange. Josiah Gist died shortly after he had become High Sheriff in 1834.

2 Hon. George Gustavus Chetwynd-Talbot, born in 1810, was rector of   Withington for 62 years.

returning from a   Northern Factory Circuit, and were just arrived
by the Bath coach from Birmingham, which was to set them down
at Prinknash Park gate.

September 28th, 1837

An escape took place from the Stow Workhouse last night: a
blind sailor having eloped with a female pauper who has left behind
her two bastard children. In the present unfinished state of the new
workhouse the parties had found an opportunity of communicating
with each other. But these are daily lessening so that in a day or two
their project would have been baffled by additional locks and bars.
In the course of the night each stole from their respective
dormitories ... and both escaped. I gave instructions to the police to
look out for the runaways. The woman has left her two children
chargeable and has therefore committed a felony and an act of
vagrancy.

October 10th, 1837

About 8 o'clock accompanied my wife and son to Mrs.
Chamberlayne's dance at Maugersbury. About fifty formed the
circle. The amusements were one whist table, a little music and a
good deal of dancing with a very elegant and expensive supper and
French wines, etc. The party was pronounced agreeable, the host
and hostess very courteous, the music indifferent, at least the
quadrille band. The company consisted of Lord Redesdale and
Miss Mitford, Sir C. and Lady Imhoff and a Baron Soden, who
accompanied them and who is a great nephew of the late Mrs.
Hastings, an unhealthy looking young man, speaking only
German, my little remaining skill in that language being brought
into play to converse with him. He has come to receive Mrs.
Hasting's legacy. It is understood that Governor Warren Hastings
left everything in his widow's power, and she has left Daylesford
estate with the mansion, furniture, etc. to her son Sir C. Imhoff,
for his life, afterwards to be sold, and the proceeds divided between
her German nieces, one of which is Mrs. Winter, wife of the rector
of Daylesford and formerly Marie Chapuset. (After this digression
it would be too tedious to return to Mr. and Mrs. Chamberlayne's
other guests, except to say that Edward had eyes only for his
Sophy, particularly as he had to return to Oxford the following
day.)

November 6th, 1837

Drove Margaret to Daylesford to call on our old friends Winter and Marie (Chapuset) in their new character of man and wife. The lady was at home. Winter came in from hunting, alas! that the clergy should persist in the practise!

December 15th, 1837

Looked in at the church at Stow to view an altar-piece lately presented by Mr. Chamberlayne. It is really a fine picture of the Crucifixion by Gaspar Creyer, a Flemish painter, contemporary of Rubens. It will be necessary to entirely block up the east window and to introduce another window on the north side of the chancel to throw a proper light on to the picture. W. Chamberlayne purchased this picture in Flanders. The expense of framing and fixing it, and making the necessary alterations in the chancel will be defrayed by Mr. Hippisley as patron and Vavasour as rector.

January 3rd, 1838

Went to the Tolsey (in Gloucester) to attend the second general meeting of the subscribers to the Gloucester and Bristol Diocesan Church Building Association, as relates to the archdeaconry of Gloucester. The Bishop took the chair. It appears that about £13,000 have been subscribed in the whole Diocese, of which the clergy have subscribed about £4,000. Various churches to be built, or enlarged, have been promised aid from the Society, among them the enlargement of Horsley[1] has been decided on. A church is to be built in the parish of Leckhampton,[2] another contiguous to Gloucester in the parish of Hempsted, [3] which will be of great service to the population rapidly accumulating about the docks. Lysons is to be minister, which will enable him to live in his own mansion at Hempsted, and to be non-resident at Rodmarton the climate of which he considers to be prejudicial to his health.

A church in the populous part of the parish of Stroud is likely to be erected.[4] The prospect is not so certain of a church being built at Purton, a hamlet of Berkeley, Lord Segrave being opposed. The

1 Rebuilt, except the tower, in 1838-9 by Thomas Rickman.
2 By E.G. Shellard; but replaced by the present St. Philip & St. James in 1870.
3 Hempsted church is medieval.
4 Holy Trinity, 1838 by Thomas Foster.

Bishop urged the claims of the association earnestly and at considerable length; but he is a hesitating public speaker, not very effective. A series of resolutions were moved and seconded by Archdeacon Trimbrill, Sir George Prevost, etc. The best speech was by Powell, incumbent of Stroud, an able man and pleasing orator, who dilated on the small amounts of subscriptions as compared with the opulence of the diocese, and on the importance of an endowment fund, without which the building of churches was only a one-sided labour of love. The Bishop, in reply, argued that if it were necessary to wait till endowments were ready, the good work must be postponed indefinitely.

January 5th, 1838

A hoar frost and misty morning, preceding a very fine winter's day, the mist hanging in the low valleys, the sun shining brightly on the tops of the hills. Walked from Prinknash with Howell and his son Frederick to Painswick Lodge to call on Hyett,[1] who is suffering from a bad attack of gout, which however does not impair his natural energy. Enjoyed two or three hours conversation on all manner of topics, many very interesting; the political relations of the country, the parties in Parliament, the insurrection in Lower Canada, the local politics of the county, statistical matters in respect of trade and manufacture, the treatment of pauper lunatics, the subject of lunacy at large, the opinions entertained by Newman, Pusey, Keble, etc. Hyett is a talented man with a mind quickly alive to public affairs, and doubtless not disinclined to resume a place in parliament, should an opportunity offer. His opinions have altered since he represented Stroud on its first being entitled to return a member under the Reform Act. Bred up in Whig principals and an adherent of the Berkeley interest in the county, he soon saw reason to form an unfavourable opinion of the section to which he was attached, when he came to act on the stage of the House of Commons, and he is now decidedly Conservative in his political views.

---

1 William Henry Hyett, F.R.S. of Painswick House where he passed more than fifty years of his life. Born 1795. M.P. for Stroud 1832-3. Died 1877. Painswick House was built for Charles Hyett, between 1733 and 1738. W.H. Hyett employed George Basevi to make additions to the house. W.H. Hyett's son was Sir Francis Hyett, the Gloucestershire historian, who lived to be over 90.

January 6th, 1838

A hard frost, with a cold raw rime or fog, which the sun could not disperse. Left Prinknash about 11 o'clock on my return home, by Birdlip and Andoversford, where I baited, and passed half an hour with the Dean of Gloucester's youngest son, John, lately entered Exeter College, rather a promising youth. He was baiting also, being on his road from Oddington to Gloucester, whither the Dean and the rest of his family had gone yesterday to enter on their usual residence.

January 9th, 1838

A hard frost, easterly wind and cold day; light snow falling so as to cover the ground but not deep. Walked to Eyford; administered the Sacrament to A. Watts, an estimable old parishioner, now become very feeble and perhaps approaching her end. Mrs. Dolphin very kindly interested about her, met me there, and partook of the Communion with the old villager.

February 9th, 1838

Left home to meet Ford at Lower Slaughter Turnpike gate at a quarter past 4 o'clock, who had promised to convey me to Northwick Park. We travelled together in his phaeton. The drive to Blockley from Lord Northwick's lodge at the end of what was Bourton Hill, before the enclosure on the Worcester road, was new to me and in summer would be very umbrageous and pretty. It is a long descent through woods and at the foot of the valley is Dovedale, a small house belonging to Lord N. at the entrance to Blockley, with a miniature lawn, lake, island, waterfall and some flourishing evergreens, now occupied by Mr. W. Gist and his lady. It was nearly 6 o'clock when we reached Northwick Park, and when we had changed our dress, were introduced to a large party, including Lord Deerhurst, resident at Bourton-on-the-Hill with his lady, daughter of the late Sir C. Cockerell and niece of Lord Northwick; His Lordship is son of the Earl of Coventry, miserably deaf, and blind in one eye, which he unfortunately lost by a random shot from his friend, and now brother-in-law, Sir C. Cockerell.

We were sumptuously entertained on plate with an excellent dinner, good wines, and courteous and friendly reception. There was general conversation on politics, all being Conservatives, and more privately between myself and Mr. Kennaway, Vicar of Campden, who is apparently a very amiable pious man, bred up among the evangelical clergy, but moderate, and now disposed I should say to keep a middle course between that party and the High Church section owing Pusey and Newman as their leaders, and at present exercising no small influence — probably to good — in the Church. Ford and myself slept at Northwick.

February 20th, 1838
Lord Northwick met his clerical guests at an early breakfast in the library at 9 o'clock, having first conducted us into his picture gallery and given us a cursory view of his treasures. We never left him till past 3 o'clock, the time being most agreeably consumed in inspecting his collections, in going over his spacious mansion, and in varied conversation chiefly connected with the fine arts and observations arising out of Lord N's foreign travel in early life. Lord Northwick is a singular character, about 67 years of age, proud of his ancient family and Norman descent, a high Tory, a strong aristocrat, a political gentleman of a past school, with much of the manners of a foreigner; he speaks vehemently with much gesticulation, and loves patient listeners provided they show an interest in the subject, and are to a certain extent acquainted with it. One excuses egotism and a little love of flattery when there is so much of interest to be communicated; but he is little conversant with many matters the knowledge of which would make him a useful character. He has not applied his mind to the duties of the magistracy or the administration of country business.

Northwick Park has a large herd of deer, a fine sheet of water, a prospect over rich and fertile land. The house, which has been very much improved by the present possessor, is sufficiently antiquated being of the date of the architectural Earl of Burlington whose style and designs were adopted.1

February 24th, 1838
Very heavy rain and a rapid thaw led to a more decided flood for some hours than I have ever observed in this valley. The bridges

1 The east front was remodelled by Lord Burlington in 1732. The picture gallery was added in 1832 by this Lord Northwick, who, Howard Colvin thinks, employed the local builder Richard Hulls.

over the brook were nearly submerged, the direct access to the lower part of the village was impeded, and many cottages, gardens and yards were under water.

February 26th, 1838

Wrote to the Secretary of State for the Colonies on behalf of the Smith family of Eyford to enquire about emigration to New South Wales. The enquiry was suggested in a letter from Sam Smith who emigrated about a year ago, accepting an invitation from a Colonist from the neighbourhood of Cheltenham, named Arkell, [1] now advanced in life, who has acquired a valuable property in land, stock, etc., and wished for a young Gloucestershire farmer to come out to assist him in cultivating his property in the interior of Bathurst county. Sam Smith has been cordially received and is now engaged to marry the daughter of Arkell. He considers himself on the high road to prosperity, and wishes members of his own family to follow his example, and desires them to send out to him four married labourers with families whom Arkell will engage, and also a carpenter.

April 23rd, 1838

In Cheltenham found time to make a circuit round the new part of the town beyond Montpellier, Lansdown Place, Crescent, Villas, etc. which I had never before gone through so thoroughly. The town is increasing wonderfully in that direction with some very spacious and handsome residences, rows of large houses suitable for people of considerable affluence and other ranges of smaller houses for families of smaller size and means. The Bayshill estate is also about to be laid out as building ground on a like extensive and ornamental scale. The new hotel, the Queen's Hotel, [2] now in progress of erection at the upper end of Sherborne Walk is a very fine building on an immense scale.

1 Arkell is a well-known Gloucestershire name. A John Arkell died at Boddington near Cheltenham in 1818.
2 Built by the brothers Robert and Charles Jearrad.

May 8th, 1838

During my absence a young Oxonian, Mr. Wright of Christ Church called with a friend at Upper Slaughter to see the *Thlaspi perfoliatum.* They were received by my wife who sent the gardener to guide the young botanists to the locality where it grows, which done the young men returned delighted with their pilgrimage. The history of this plant is singular. It is a very humble herb of the spring. The old Oxford botanist, Bobart, nearly a century ago, discovered it on some downs near Burford, and on his authority it has been retained in botanical works as an indigenous plant; but by all botanists sought in vain in its alleged habitat, so that at length it has been generally supposed that old Bobart was in error, and that the plant was really not of British growth. In fact the breaking up of the old downland near Burford had long extirpated it.

However three years ago my son discovered it growing in profusion on some stony banks in this parish, at the back of my rectory farm and in an adjacent field, where the plough never had reached, nor can reach. He transmitted to the Botanical Garden at Oxford specimens which have since been cultivated there, and has the credit of reintroducing it into the British Flora. The curator of the Oxford Botanic Garden, Baxter, being engaged in a periodical work on English Botany has given a plate of the *Thlaspi perfoliatum,* with letter press supplied by my son, whose name very frequently occurs in the same elegant work as the authority for other rare plants of indigenous growth which he has found in various localities, especially in this district. Another habitat has been found for the *Thlaspi perfoliatum* by Edward on Fosse Bridge Hill, on the side of the road to Cirencester.

May 19th, 1838

Received a letter from the Postmaster at Moreton-in-Marsh announcing a change in the Post Office arrangements there which will prove inconvenient to us, as far as relates to the letters from Gloucester, Cheltenham, Tewkesbury and parts of the North — which, I am afraid, will practically now reach us only on the second day after they are dispatched.

May 23rd, 1838

In the evening Billingsley walked over with two fine boys, his nephews, to shoot some rooks.

June 20th, 1838 (Mr. Howell was staying at Upper Slaughter)

Towards 5 o'clock Frederick Howell arrived on horse-back from Prinknash in obedience to a summons sent in a letter from his father by yesterday's post. He is much grown, a fine intelligent lad of eighteen. He is destined for the medical profession, to be brought up as a surgeon at King's College, London.

June 21st, 1838

Howell *père* accompanied me in the open carriage to Stow, whence he proceeded on foot to Chipping Norton to visit a mill there, and returned chiefly on foot but partly by the *Novelty* coach to Stow, and accompanied me home to dinner in the phaeton. Frederick rode to Whichford[1] to call on my son and returned in the evening having found the curate and Sophy quite well, and much pleased with his reception.

June 22nd, 1838

Howell left in our phaeton, driven by my servant to within a mile of Blockley, whither he proceeded on foot to visit the silk mills there and to walk from there to Campden and Broadway for a like visitation. At Broadway he proposed to sleep. Frederick remained with us till after dinner so that he might enjoy a few hours fishing; but he was inexpert or the day unsuitable, for he returned empty handed and left us about 7 p.m. on his horse to join his father at Broadway.

June 28th, 1838

A very fine day. Auspicious weather for the Queen's Coronation, which was celebrated generally with great spirit and zeal. Great preparations at Stow for doing the due honour of the day, and an exhibition of loyalty by distribution of the good things of life to the poor, and provide a dinner for 400 in the market place; beef, mutton, beer, etc: I returned home to dinner, and shortly afterwards Margaret and I distributed cake and cheese, and beer to about 40 children of our Free School and Sunday School,

---

1 Edward was now married to Sophy Vavasour and was for a short time curate at Whichford in Oxfordshire.

and a party of 15 or 16 sat down in my servants' hall to a substantial Coronation supper, the partakers of the good cheer being our servants, haymakers, labourers, and the masters and mistress of the parish schools. The farmers gave treats to the rest of the villages.

July 4th, 1838

Wrote to Wadham College[1] to furnish them with the particulars of the vicarage at Painswick, the advowson of which is now on sale, in case they should be disposed to become the purchasers. I have obtained the details yesterday from Mr. Hyett. An Act of Parliament has just been obtained to enable the trustees of this benefice to sell it, and to vest the money in funds, the dividends to be applied to diminish the burden of poor rates in the parish. The object has been to do away with the evil of a popular election of a vicar on each vacancy. The ratepayers having a suffrage, disorder, drunkenness and all the concommitments of a contested election, with great expense in agency, treating and the like, has hitherto been the rule of the place.

August 22nd, 1838

The Bishop arrived at the Unicorn Inn at Stow from Campden, where he had confirmed and visited yesterday, complaining of fatigue and over-exertion and suffering from the increased infirmity of his eye-sight. He received me with his wonted friendship. When His Lordship had robed, he went to the church, where confirmation was administered to, I suppose, nearly 400 young persons of both sexes. All was done with much order and decorum. The Bishop delivered a suitable, plain but rather feeble and commonplace discourse on confirmation. The Bishop and clergy retired for an hour to the Rectory. Several ladies were present; Mrs. Leigh of Stoneleigh Abbey with a daughter who has been confirmed. My son and daughter who were greeted by Bishop Monk with the utmost cordiality and kindness. At 2 o'clock we returned to the church for evening service. The Bishop's charge was very long and laboured; his imperfect vision led to much hesitation … his unwillingness to exhaust the attention of his hearers led him

---

1 Wadham College declined.

to curtail his charge by omitting considerable portions, and consequently the line of argument was interrupted.

Bishop Monk is a man of very kindly disposition very well meaning; but lacks judgement, and is of a very susceptible, irritable, and sensitive temperament. The evening exceedingly damp and cold; but the labours of the day not yet over as we sallied forth in our chariot to meet the Bishop at Mr. Ford's (at Little Rissington) where he was to sleep preparatory to two Confirmations fixed for to-morrow at Bourton-on-the-Water and Northleach. The Bishop adverted to a subject of some local importance as regards his now greatly extended diocese, in which there are no less than three charitable associations for affording pecuniary relief to distressed clergymen, their widows and orphans; that long established in the old diocese of Gloucester, a like association for the City of Bristol, and a third in North Wiltshire. The Bishop thinks it desirable that these should be concentrated into one; but it is obvious that such an arrangement will be fraught with many difficulties.

December 18th, 1838

Drove in the phaeton with the groom to pass a day or two at Stanway Vicarage. Looked over the premises with a view to making a list of fixtures that they may be left in the house for the use of my son. Walked with Frederick Aston to Toddington. Called on the aged vicar and his wife, whom I found very infirm and much broken. John Eddy was with his parents. To the feebleness of old age has been superadded the misery of the son, a clergyman and his father's curate at Didbrook and Hailes, marrying a low girl, daughter of the person keeping the Turnpike gate at Stump's Cross, once his father's housemaid. And the daughter has disgraced herself by a clandestine marriage with one Pounce, formerly a handsome footman to Lady Elcho in which capacity he served when Miss Eddy first saw him. He wore the Duke of Newcastle's livery when she married him.

December 19th, 1838

A hard frost on the hills, a fine seasonable day. After breakfast left Stanway for home. Frederick Aston walked with me through Church Stanway to Stumps Cross Turnpike gate where we parted. I reached Upper Slaughter by two; busy afterwards in superintending the planting out of evergreens and other shrubs in the pleasure ground. Found Margaret and her mother much as usual.

December 4th, 1838

I spent an hour at the Workhouse, inspecting all the records, detecting some irregularities, reproving and advising different parties, the Governor and Matron not excepted.

December 20th, 1838

A very full meeting of Guardians at the Workhouse. This was the day for entering into contracts with trades-people for bread, meat, groceries, etc.

January 2nd, 1839

Attended the annual meeting for the Archdeaconry of Gloucester of the Diocesan Society for the building and endowing of churches. Two churches, at Leckhampton and Horsley, to which the society have allotted £1200, are in progress. Bathurst has given £950 towards the endowment of a church at Cinderford[1] in the Forest of Dean, where a populous hamlet has sprung up of late years in consequence of the large collieries and ironworks in that quarter. The proposed church is to be aided by a grant from the funds of the Diocesan association, and Dr. Warneford has promised £500 towards the erection of a parsonage.

Dr. Warneford has further devoted £2500 towards the endowment of five churches. He is indeed a magnificent donor. God has blessed him with very extensive means, and his taste leads him to indulge in public charities and so after careful consideration of each case, he disposes of thousands in a twelvemonth, not to mention assistance given by loans to struggling tradesmen and others. Leamington is indebted to him mainly for a hospital, Oxford for a lunatic asylum. His own churches of Bourton-on-the-Hill and Moreton-in-Marsh have been repaired, enlarged and pewed, and schools built and endowed at both places. The Bishop's chaplain moved a vote of thanks to Dr. Warneford. I said a few emphatic words in his praise, congratulating myself on my intimacy with two such men as him and Bathurst.

---

1 St. John's by Edward Blore.

From the Tolsey I returned into Court, and attended on Trials
for felony, etc. till it was time to dress for dinner at the Palace,
whither I repaired soon after 6 o'clock. We had a large party,
chiefly of clergy with some ladies, and much civility from the
Bishop and Mrs. Monk; but the tone of the party was not
particularly social or cheerful.

January 3rd, 1839

After breakfast at the Bell, accompanied Bathurst to the opening
of his Court, and remained there or in Purnell's Court the greater
part of the forenoon. In Purnell's Court two trials took place of
prisoners whom I had committed, two young men for picking a
pocket at Stow Fair were sentenced to four months imprisonment
each. Left Gloucester for Prinknash Park where I was most
cordially received.

January 4th, 1839

A good deal of rain had fallen during the night; but the day was
fine and clear and sunny and the prospect over the Vale of Severn
exceedingly striking, at times brilliantly lighted up. We did not go
beyond the limits of the park, strolling in the plantations, on the
terrace, etc: but chiefly conversing in Howell's study on all manner
of topics. In the evening Hyett joined us ... He had brought his lady
and children, to whom were added the young people from Upton
St. Leonards Rectory — children of Mr. Parsons, who with the
Howell tribe made up a nice little circle of dancers. How much
more sensible than the elaborate *recherché* and long protracted
children's balls so much in vogue!

January 5th, 1839

When I rose early there was a white world. Emmeline Howell
prepared for me an early breakfast; before I had concluded, her
father appeared and accompanied me to the Park gate to meet the
Stroud coach on its way to Cheltenham. I could not get an inside
place and found the weather very inclement, particularly as we
descended Cooper's Hill in a heavy storm of mingled snow, sleet,
and rain.

January 9th, 1839

I was tempted to take a little walking exercise in the vineyards and pleasure ground after luncheon.

March 1st, 1839

Rode to Northleach under the commission of the Bishop to survey the buildings on the Vicarage Glebe and report on their condition. Found the Vicarage capable of being made comfortable, though not a good house. It stands in a cheerful garden and pleasure ground, adjoining the very handsome church, in the vicinity of, but well secluded from, some mean tenements at the edge of the town and near some pleasant and commodious grass fields belonging to the glebe. There are about 180 acres of land laid out in two farms; but the farm buildings are in a sad state of dilapidation and must be entirely pulled down and rebuilt. Income about £260 per annum.

March 11th, 1839

To Wyck Rissington and left my card for Mr. Crompton, the curate, a Cambridge man ordained deacon at Christmas last, who is represented to be a pleasing, energetic, well-informed man and a zealous adherent of the Newman and Pusey school of divinity. He was from home.

March 19th, 1839

Considerable annoyance in consequence of the absence of our gardener, J. Smith, who has left the village because of being over head and ears in debt, leaving behind his wife and family. He had given me no hint of his intention and his absence is very inconvenient; but after this proceeding he can hardly return into my service, indeed he has sold nearly all his household goods. He was a careless, thoughtless man, with a poor helpmate, not a stout labourer, but a handyman acquainted with many useful things as to agriculture and gardening, and useful in his place.

March 26th, 1839

Engaged superintending gardening operations having determined to try J. Andrews, a decent labourer, in the place which John Smith has deserted.

April 3rd, 1839

A note from Mr. Pegler of Bledington with additional particulars as to the pedigree of a cow which he has procured for me and which is one of a lot recently imported into this neighbourhood from Cumberland being a very superior stock, descended from the famous bull Comet. She is a noble animal, very poor and travel-worn, likely to calve in less than a month, and worthy to range with my two admired cows, and likely to keep up the reputation I have somehow gained, of being a breeder of singularly fine stock. A three year old in-calf heifer, which I lately sold for £30, has made a considerable noise, as the finest animal bred for many years in this district. I gave £25 for my Cumberland cow.

April 3rd, 1839

A letter from M. Gantheron, the Swiss gentleman in whose favour I was asked some time ago to use my little influence in Gloucester, where he was about to settle as a teacher of languages. He complains that his prospects there are very bad and asks me whether removal to Stow with the same ends in view would be likely to better them; alas! poor man.

April 10th, 1839

An adjournment in the Court took place, therefore Bathurst, Hale, Barwick Baker[1], Curtis Hayward and myself went to the Cathedral, chiefly to look at the classical and elegant monument lately erected to the memory of our late worthy Gaoler, Cunningham, at the expense of several old magistrates which, as to inscription, taste, etc. is chiefly the doing of Bathurst. Sauntered for some time examining and discussing the architectural antiquities so familiar to us all, then lounged in a bookseller's shop, turning over old books and works of art.

---

1 All well-known county names. Barwick Lloyd-Baker was himself commemorated in the Cathedral by an elaborate monument by W.S. Frith in 1886.

April 25th, 1839

Very fine spring weather. Rode to Bledington: surveyed the parsonage, as I had been requested that I might be able to certify that it is an unfit residence for a clergyman.

Called at Mr. H. Pegler's, who was from home; but looked over his yards, to see the cattle, especially a fine bull and some cows and stirks which were part of the recent importation from Cumberland by which I profited.

April 29th, 1839

A continuance of the same fine weather. Visiting sick and afflicted parishioners. Rode to Stow. Called on the Rev. Mr. Allen and signed a certificate that the glebe house at his living at Bledington was on account of its meanness unsuitable as a residence for the incumbent, so that he might obtain from the Bishop licence for non-residence.

April 30th, 1839

Soon after breakfast I was visited by two professional men, by whom I was served with an Order from the House of Lords to attend on Monday 6th May, before the committee of Privileges and to be sworn to give evidence on the petition of James Tracy to be admitted to the title of Viscount Tracy of Rathcool, an Irish peerage and to produce as vicar of Stanway, the register books of that parish from 1656 to 1800. This gentleman claims to be the male heir of the Tracy family of Toddington, descended from a former peer of that line, which was understood to terminate in a female, daughter of the last Lord Tracy who died in 1797, the estates in Gloucestershire descending to that daughter, now the Lady Sudeley. Lord Sudeley (formerly Mr. Hanbury-Tracy) when recently elevated to the peerage adopted that title and not Tracy, in persuasion that the claimant might succeed. The estates are not claimed. The gentlemen left money with me to meet the expenses of my journey to London. Disliking to travel by night, which I must do, if I perform my own duty on Sunday, I rode to Lower Swell and secured Perkins's services for that day.

May 4th, 1839

Delightful weather. After an early breakfast left home by 8 o'clock on my way to London, going to Northleach in my open carriage. Arrived more than a quarter of an hour earlier than the *Magnet* and went to the Vicarage to shake hands with my friends there Mr. and Mrs. Aston and young Frederick who with his father accompanied me to the Inn, and remained with me till the coach left. I had no companion inside the coach. We stopped for luncheon at Oxford, and reached the station house on the Great Western Railway at or near Maidenhead a little before 5 o'clock. The station is at the twenty fifth milestone from London. The railroad is carried on a very high embankment across the meadows between Maidenhead and Bray. I believe it will soon be completed as far as Twyford. The coach drove into the station yard where the passengers alighted, leaving their luggage with the coach which proceeds a little onwards and reaches the level of the railway by a road constructed for the purpose. There the carriages are placed each on a railway truck, ready to be hooked on to the train when it comes to that point. Meantime the passengers receive a railway ticket to London which purports to be worth 5s\6d.We arrived ten minutes before the hour of starting. There is much less bustle than at the Birmingham — Manchester railroad stations and no appearance of the transit of merchandize as yet. The railway is also on a different construction from those on which I have hitherto travelled, the width between the rails being 7 ft. and consequently the coaches are as wide, each holding eight persons, or four in two breadths. The distance to Paddington 22 miles is traversed in 50 mins. including stoppages. The coach in which I travelled held only myself and Mr. Palmer, M.P. for Berkshire, a very pleasant gentlemanly person. At the Paddington station the coach is met by a pair of horses, the passengers resume their seats, and the journey is continued by the Edgeware Road to Oxford Street, and I took a coach at the Green Man and proceeded to Ibbetson's Hotel, Vere Street, a quiet orderly place with good quiet sleeping rooms. Dinner and tea and to bed.

May 6th, 1839

I found that I should be sworn today but not examined till to-morrow. The claimant's pretensions are thus based — that Edward the 2nd Viscount Tracy who died in 1662 had a son Robert, Judge of the common pleas, settled at Coscomb, who died and was buried at Didbrook in 1735 — that this Judge Tracy's third son settled in Dublin, of whom there is no trace in any of the family documents of the Tracys of Toddington or Stanway, or in any existing pedigrees. When I had deposited my Stanway registers in my room at Ibbetsons's I proceeded to call at Lord Wemyss's. Lady W. was full of the Tracy peerage affair, the claimant having waited on Lord W. and urged his Lordship to give evidence as to the extinction of the male line of the Stanway branch (Lady Elcho having been the Tracy heiress). Acting on the advice of his solicitor Lord. W. has gone to take the oaths, which he had omitted doing during this Queen's reign. From Stratford Place I went to Connaught Terrace to call on the Misses Guydickens whom I found *bien portant,* and glad to see me. Here too the conversation chiefly turned on the claim to the Tracy peerage which, these descendants of the old Tracys better versed than myself in the traditions of the house from which maternally we are sprung, held in considerable scorn and disbelief.

May 7th, 1839

I reached the House before 2 o'clock. There seemed to be difficulty in mustering sufficient number of peers to form a Committee of Privileges at which seven peers must be present. In the lobby was the claimant Mr. Tracy a middle-aged man with a strong Irish accent.

It was intimated that .... there were clergymen from the country with parochial registers to be produced, whose detention in town would be inconvenient, and they should be examined and dismissed. I was further asked whether I had known the last Viscount Tracy. I replied that I had not known him though I did know his descendants. On being asked whether I meant Lady Sudeley and her children I answered in the affirmative. As I returned from the House of Lords I deviated into Downing Street, to the Foreign Office in hope of a friendly interview with John Backhouse. At length he came to me in a very hurried manner to explain it was impossible for him to see me, as in consequence of the defeat of the Ministry on the Jamaica question, they had resigned office, having just been with the Queen to tender their resignations. Of course I retired quickly,pleased to learn there was a prospect of a firm Conservative administration. At 7 o'clock I went to dinner at Lord Wemyss's. The conversation turned much on the change of administration as well as the Tracy peerage.[1]

1 In 1848 the claimant's case was declared fraudulent.

May 20th, 1839

A fine balmy air, mild and growing, mostly overclouded but with bright gleams. Wrote to Rodwell for a supply of books to the Stow Book Society. Drove Margaret to Northleach to call on the Astons. It proved to be the Feast Day of one or more Friendly Societies, and after performing divine service and preaching, Frederick Aston and his son had gone to dinner with members of the club, but came to us when Mrs. A. apprized them that we were at the vicarage. We made a long visit inspecting the house, garden and church. The latter is a very spacious, lofty, elegant structure, highly enriched with lofty tower, elaborate porch, tall windows full of light tracery and battlemented, pinnacled, with niches, statues, and carving, probably of the date of Henry VII, at least chiefly of the fifteenth century, the south aisle exhibiting the date 1489. The piety of wealthy clothiers and woolstaplers was displayed in the erection of this fair parish church, and those like Campden, Burford, and Chipping Norton. But now from all these places, all or nearly all vestiges of the ancient occupation and prosperity have disappeared, and the valleys about Stroud, with more copious streams and cheaper supply of coal, have long superseded these hill-towns. Elaborate monumental brasses attest their opulence, especially of one Forty, one of the chief founders or restorers of the church. The church has been recently repewed with deal, but not in a very appropriate manner. There is a barrel organ, and some modern benefactor has expended a considerable sum with bad taste in a paltry, incongruous altar-piece. We returned home by Farmington, calling at the Lodge, but Mr. Waller was from home, and Mrs. W. gone out airing.

June 17th, 1839

Accompanied my wife in the chariot to Cheltenham. Walked to look at the splendid hotel called "the Queen's", and the projected, and already in part commenced, improvements on the Bay's Hill estate, which it is planned to lay out in ranges of building, crescents, parades, squares or detached villas for residences of a superior grade: the design when accomplished will be very handsome. Near Bay's Hill House, on the crown of the hill is the hamlet of Alstone, a very handsome Gothic church is nearly completed.[1] Not far from this, a house has been selected as a

1 Christ Church, 1838-40, by R. and C. Jearrad.

residence for Mr. Close, the Perpetual Curate and Incumbent of Cheltenham, whose vast popularity and influence daily increase, insomuch that I believe, more than £2,000 have been subscribed by his devoted adherents to purchase, fit up and furnish, and present to him this house which he had selected for his future abode, intending to rent it of the proprietor. We returned through the extensive nursery grounds of Jessop the principal gardener, an enterprising character and one of the leaders of the Cheltenham Tea-totallers.

July 16th, 1839

A very beautiful day. After breakfast (at Wood Stanway) a very pleasant walk through the fields with my son to Hailes, the ruins of the abbey,[1] village, etc. After luncheon we drove to Winchcombe and Sudeley Castle, and explored the latter ruin. My wife accompanied Edward in his phaeton. I drove Sophy in ours.

August 11th, 1839

The newspapers communicate the distressing tidings of an affliction which has befallen my cousin Lady Cornewall:[2] her second daughter, in her 17th year, while amusing herself at Moccas Court, with her brother, in a boat on the Wye, fell over, and though the body was found within a few minutes life could not be restored. We had lately heard that the eldest daughter was engaged

---

1 In the National Trust Museum at Hailes we can see some of the Chapter House bosses close to, and marvellously preserved they are. There is also part of the arm from Edmund Earl of Cornwall's effigy, and elegant bits of a shrine; but compared with what must have been destroyed they are almost as nothing. The plan of the monastic buildings can be traced on the ground, and Kip's and Buck's drawings, which are shown, help to explain it, and show how the Tracy family's house was built on the west side of the cloisters, after the Reformation. The way to enjoy the site is to pretend that the walls rise up around us, and to be careful therefore not to walk through a solid wall by stepping over a foundation. To Francis and Edward Witts it must have been a romantic ruin, particularly the remains of the Tracys' house.

The wall paintings in the little church are some of the best in Gloucestershire and include a secular coursing scene (out of Queen Mary's Psalter of 1308), female saints, Royal heraldry, and "Behold St. Christopher, go Thy way in Peace", a huge figure stretching from floor to roof.

2 The Cornewall family of Moccas claimed descent from Richard Earl of Cornwall, King of the Romans, and founder of Hailes Abbey.

to be married to young Master,[1] M.P. for Cirencester, son of Col.
Master of Knole Park, who will eventually succeed to the Abbey
estates at Cirencester, a connexion apparently much to be desired.

August 17th, 1839

A letter received from Mr. Chamberlayne from Cheltenham,
where he now is with his family, in which he explains that he has
resolved on withdrawing for a few years from the neighbourhood,
and letting his place at Maugersbury, alledging as a reason the
severity of the climate. He might have added that Mrs.
Chamberlayne sighs for the society to be enjoyed only in or near a
public place, and is dreadfully *ennuyée* with the solitude of the old
mansion near Stow, and the infrequency of social engagements in
its vicinity.

July 1st, 1840

To the Court (in Gloucester) where I attended until the County
meeting was held, to address the Queen and Prince Albert on the
occasion of their providential escape from assassination. The High
Sheriff, Sir M. Hicks-Beach, presided. None of the nobility of the
County were present, being mostly now in Town, the only M.P. for
the County present, R. Hale, proposed the address to the Queen,
which was seconded by Mr. Pyrke. Col. Kingscote proposed the
address to Prince Albert, seconded by H. Waller, the motion that
the address should be entrusted to the Lord Lieutenant was
proposed by Purnell and seconded by me: thus there was an
equipoise of Conservatives and   Whigs.

July 3rd, 1840.

Walked in Cheltenham with my wife to see the Railway Station,
on the side of the old Turnpike road from Cheltenham to
Gloucester, about half a mile beyond Lansdown Place. It is yet in a
very unfinished state; but advancing towards completion. Showed
my wife, who had not previously seen any railway for locomotive

1 Thomas Chester-Master who married Catherine, granddaughter of Sir George
Cornewall, builder of Moccas, which now belongs to their descendant Richard
Chester-Master, of Cirencester.

travelling, the general arrangements, engines, first and second class carriages etc.

July 31st, 1840.

Beautiful summer weather. After breakfast rode by appointment to New Bridge, between Great Rissington and Clapton to meet Mr. Ford who was named as member of a committee of magistrates with H. Waller and myself to make a report on the reparation or rebuilding of that as a County Bridge. Waller was absent at Goodwood races. Ford brought with him his sister now on a visit at Little Rissington, his neice who is to be married on Tuesday next to a son of Sir Eardley Wilmot, and his daughters Dulcibella and Jemima. Fred and Henry Ford also rode down to the trysting point, whither also came from Gloucester, T. Fulljames, the County Surveyor, mounted on a Northleach hack. Agreed on the line to be taken, a diversion of the stream, the Windrush, the erection of a new and more commodious bridge, and an expenditure of about £200.

I rode with Fulljames on his way towards Northleach to beyond Clapton, where I parted from him and pursued my way home. Fulljames informed me that he has projected a work of art, views and illustrations of all the Gloucestershire churches, with copperplate engravings.[1]

September 13th, 1840

Beautiful weather. After an early breakfast set out in my open carriage with my servant to Stanway to perform the duties there and preach the promised sermon on the death of Lady Rossmore. The service began at 11 o'clock, and the congregation was large. The attendants from Wormington Grange came in three carriages. Mr. Gist, with, I think, three other gentlemen and three ladies occupied the pew belonging to the Mansion House; there were at least nine or ten other persons in deep mourning, male and female, whether any of them were above the rank of domestics of the Gist family or of Lord and Lady Rossmore I had no means of judging. When the Service was over and at the churchyard gate I was accosted in a friendly manner by Mr. Gist who explained that his

---

1Perhaps this was wishful thinking? This Fulljames was uncle to the architect of the same name.

lady [1] was absent from being slightly indisposed, and a middle aged gentleman, a Mr. Lewis, Irish from his accent, whom I understood to be a relation of Lord Rossmore addressed me in his Lordship's name in set phrases of politeness and thanks, requesting me to call on his Lordship when I came to Cheltenham. The mourning party then withdrew, and I returned to the vicarage for luncheon.

September 22nd, 1840

My chief business (in Cheltenham) was to wait on Lord Rossmore. I found the old peer in a calmer state and more resigned that I had been led to expect. He looks well for his years, his bald head enveloped in a kind of handkerchief, sitting in an easy chair, with his legs laid on another. Two gentlemen to whom I was introduced, were sitting with him, the name of one escaped me, and the other, I believe was Mr. Lewis but not the gentleman of that name I met at Stanway. The conversation turned chiefly on the excellent qualities of the deceased, and the blunders that had been made at the time of her funeral which he imputed to Mr. Gist. He seemed well pleased with the report of my sermon and asked if I had any intention of printing it. I replied that I had never yet printed any of my sermons and begged to be excused.

December 1st, 1840

Drove my wife on a little excursion to Buckland to inspect the church there as interesting and curious in respect of architecture and antiquity. Ecclesiastical architecture engages my son's attention greatly at present, his mind having been drawn in that direction by observations made on foreign churches on the Continent. He and Sophy accompanied us on horseback. Buckland is a retired village in a dell under the hills extending from Stanway towards Broadway, looking at this season as little to advantage as possible; but it must have great attractions in summer, among fine timber trees, and surrounded by rich meadows and pastures. The property is chiefly in the hands of Sir Thomas Phillipps of Middle Hill. Buckland is in Gloucestershire and was anciently the property of the Thynnes, probably a branch of the noble family of Bath.

The church is on a bank, where the valley is contracted between two wooded hills. Close behind is the ancient gable-ended

1 Mrs. Mary Ann Gist was sister to Lord Rossmore.

whitewashed, half ruinous spacious old mansion, now occupied as a farmhouse with a courtyard in front, and short avenue leading from the village road. The church porch is on the north. A very striking feature occurs on opening the door viz. on the left, formed out of the wall, a holy water stoup, in excellent preservation.[1]

August 30th, 1841

Reached Cirencester, and finding a train ready to start determined on taking that route.[2] Our chariot was soon adjusted on a truck, and ourselves seated in a first class coach, our man servant in a second class carriage. Distance from Cirencester to Swindon 18 miles, some high embankments, some deep cuttings, one long tunnel. Harvest going on everywhere and looking beautifully rich. Motion not easy, much bumping. Speed at times very considerable: on the embankments we went very slowly. All at Swindon in an unfinished state. A train came in from London to which our carriage was attached, and we steamed away for Chippenham. [3]

October 15th, 1842

Sad news awaited me on getting up, an express having arrived from Prinknash Park with a few lines written in deep distress by my poor friend Howell. [4]

Poor Howell was very grievously affected at meeting me in his bedroom, where I found him with his children Emmeline and Edward, the latter having been fetched from his tutor's Mr. Moore's at Brimpsfield. Emmeline conducts herself beautifully; deep feeling suppressed, with thoughtful solicitude, calmness and

---

1 Here Mr. Witts, like Sir John Betjeman, savours the thrill of opening the church door for a first time; but unlike Sir John, he immediately notices an antiquarian detail, and goes on to describe a "very perfect piscina" in a manner wholly typical of his period, not to mention "another corresponding .... only it has no basin, or visible contrivance for the escape of liquids, which induces a doubt whether it may not be an aumbrey".

2 Alas! there are no trains in Cirencester now.

3 There was a tremendous change in travelling conditions after about 1840. Francis Witts records that on 2 April 1841 it took him two hours to get from Stanway to Cheltenham in his open carriage; but then, for perhaps the first time, he changed into a railway carriage, and arrived in Gloucester sixteen or seventeen minutes later.

4 Mrs. Howell died giving birth to her tenth child, and Witts went to his friend at once.

tenderness. Howell received a dreadful shock, and it has told on his bodily constitution which appears deranged, and needs care ... his sense of bereavement is exceedingly agonizing ... imploring aid and acts of friendship from me. We dined together *tête à tête* for he could not command his feelings to meet all his children.

October 20th, 1842

I went through the affecting duty of baptizing the infant. It was a trying scene; the mourning father, with ten children. All bore their part during the rest of the day in subduing their own agitated feelings.

October 21st, 1842

Nothing particular occurred; the melancholy preparations for the funeral to-morrow are silently going on. Took a walk with Howell, William and Frederick (a curate and a medical student, the elder sons) and Weston Hicks (of Painswick, Howell's deputy inspector of factories) by Cranham Wood to Prinknash Rough Park, the plantation overhanging the Cheltenham and Painswick road. From the summit of the precipitous bank, which I never visited before, there is a most striking view, with a beautiful foreground; few prospects in the country excel it. A little further on, towards Cooper's Hill, the eye commands another reach equally extended, but not so diversified, both include a range from the mouth of the Wye to Evesham, with distant elevations in Monmouthshire, Herefordshire, Worcestershire, Shropshire — together with the intervening valley of the Severn and Avon, and a long sweep of Cotswold Hills.

October 22nd, 1842

Found Howell braced in spirit, and strengthened to go through the arduous and trying duty of following his beloved to the grave. Only he claimed my support during the harrowing hour. Good, kind and useful Weston Hicks continued with us. Arrived at the churchyard the sorrowing widower, resting on the friendly arms of Hicks and myself, was rather dragged than walked to the pew in the church gallery, which is commonly occupied by the Prinknash family. It overlooked the vault where the remains were to be deposited at the west end of Upton St. Leonards church, under the singing gallery, near the font. The two young men descended from the gallery to the margin of the vault; it seemed better that their father, who shook with agitation and joined in the service with deep inward feeling, should not go down from his pew where Hicks and I remained to support him. The service ended, we resumed out seats in the church and returned to Prinknash.[1]

August 17th, 1847

A letter from P.B. Purnell, inviting me to his house on 24th to meet Mr. and Mrs. Lysons at dinner and to sleep, and on the following day to view the site of the Roman villa which he has been disinterring on his grounds at Stancombe Park, and which he proposed to open to public inspection on three days, receiving on the last day at a *dejeuner* all those friends and acquaintance who may favour him with their company. The remains are not remarkable for tesselated pavements, but chiefly for their extent, covering six acres, and exhibiting in the foundations the whole arrangement of a Roman mansion and its appendages. Even the road to the front door can be traced, and the ancient well remains with its original stone walling. Purnell is not famous for his hospitality, and his place enjoys many recommendations as the residence of a man of good fortune and virtue, situated in a beautiful part of the country. I regretted therefore my inability to accept, as it is the day the Bishop and his chaplain are to be our guests at Upper Slaughter.

---

1 Four years later, in 1846, Howell sold Prinknash to Mr. Ackers, and went to live in London. The baby Macleod Howell died of epilepsy in 1851.

When Thomas Dyer-Edwardes who had bought Prinknash from Mr. Ackers, died in 1928 he was converted to the Roman Catholic faith almost on his death bed and desired to leave Prinknash to the Benedictines of Caldey Island. His wishes were carried out by his grandson the Earl of Rothes, and Prinknash Park became Prinknash Abbey. It already had a monastic connection since it was a possession of St. Peter's Abbey, Gloucester before the Reformation, and was used by Abbot Parker as a country residence, and had been a grange and hunting lodge since c.1300.

The old house is on an H-shaped plan enlarged c.1514, with additions of 1870, made during the occupation of the Ackers family, and stone gateways, leading to the east and west courts erected in 1900 to celebrate the marriage of Noëlle, Countess of Rothes. The monks occupied the house with its chapel for the next thirty years; but only ten years after their arrival they had already asked Mr. H.S. Goodhart-Rendel for designs for a new Abbey.

August 31st, 1847

This day at Gloucester had been fixed for the consecration of the district church of St. Mark's, built near the Kingsholme Turnpike, by the side of the road leading to Tewkesbury and for the accommodation of a large and poor contiguous population. I walked as far as the church, but could not enter it, the door being closed as the communion was in course of administration, after the Consecration, to the Bishop and Clergy and others who remained for that sacred rite. Mr. Edward Niblett,[1] son of Mr. N., the magistrate, my old acquaintance, is the architect, and the design does him great credit. The style is Early English, very chaste, and pleasing, with a striking look of newness; being built of freestone it wore the appearance of a huge model of biscuit china.

October 12th, 1847

Stanton church is ancient, with a beautifully tapering spire: at present in a transition state for Mr. W.H. Bloxsome has, at his own expense, done much and well towards rearranging the interior, with open sittings; but has given great offence to his parishioners by taking down a singing gallery without their consent. We returned to Stanway meeting dear Sophy with Broome on his pony. Sophy got into the carriage, and her dear boy[2] cantered by or before us as we returned.

October 19th, 1847

Breakfasted with Purnell and accompanied him to Court. The usual average attendance of Magistrates, among them the Lord Lieutenant and his recreant brother, Grantley Berkeley. They glowered at each other; but there was no hostile outbreak. There does not appear to be any relaxation in the feud raging in the house of Berkeley. Lord Fitzhardinge cannot comprehend that his influence in the county is lessened by his immoralities. He cannot stomach the rejection of his brother Craven Berkeley by the electors of Cheltenham, and of his cousin and nominee, Grenville Berkeley by a combination of Conservatives, acting with the

---

1 Usually called Francis; but the names Edward and Francis in the Witts family seem almost interchangeable, and so perhaps he made a mistake.

2 Witts's grandson a very attractive boy and the apple of his grandfather's eye in his old age.

radicals who have rebelled against him, and mediated the ejection of Grantley by petition to the House of Commons. These two profligate brothers expose and fight against each other.

February 22nd, 1848

In the course of the evening Lord S. and S.[1] opened to me the very anxious position in which he has been placed by the necessity of proving his right to his title before a Committee of the House of Lords. The matter is still pending, nor can he take his seat till it is determined in his favour. His father the Rev. Thomas Twisleton, Archdeacon of Ceylon, and a younger brother of the Lord Saye and Sele of that day, as a very young man had been gay and dissipated. Even when a pupil at Westminster he had devoted himself to private theatricals, and at an early age became entangled with an actress, whom he actually married. They had a daughter but the marriage broke down, he pursuing his studies at Oxford, and she returning to the theatre in Edinburgh. Before they were divorced however Mrs. Twisleton had a son the result of an affair with a merchant named Stein, who accepted paternity of the boy and helped educate him. Thomas Twisleton became ordained, married Frederick's mother, and eventually died. It was not till Frederick succeeded to the title on the death of his cousin, that these forgotten family histories were brought to light. Now it became necessary to prove that Mrs. Twisleton's son was not the rightful heir. Mr. Stein was discovered still living, but over eighty, and prepared to admit the truth that he considered the son to be his, and the son, now a man of fifty-two, was also found, at some sea port on the eve of embarking as a sailor in the commercial marine. He readily confirmed the statement made by Stein whom he thought to be his father.[2]

1 The Wittses gave a dinner party for the Bishop of Antigua, and their guests included the new Lord Saye and Sele, formerly Frederick Twisleton of Adlestrop.

2 This indeed proved to be the case and rector soon became Archdeacon of Hereford as well as Lord Saye and Sele and owner of Broughton Castle. In 1857 he married again, Caroline, daughter of Chandos Leigh, who had been created Lord Leigh of Stoneleigh, and perhaps the girl her mother brought to Stow for confirmation years before. A family story relates how the Archdeacon assembled all his household in the chapel at Broughton Castle before their departure to Hereford, but continued reading Isaiah for so long that his wife sent all the servants to catch the train without him.

27th March, 1848

I was driving to Cheltenham in my open carriage to take a train to London. At the foot of Dowdeswell hill I passed a coach full of convicts from Gloucester gaol going to the Northleach House of Correction, with four horses.

A little further on Lord Fitzhardinge's foxhounds were collected by the roadside ready for the chase, and as I proceeded a crowd was gathered in a wide part of the turnpike road, horsemen, foot people, and many in carriages. As I drove up, the peer rode from Cheltenham, and we met in the crowd. He recognized me with a smile, amused with the oddness of the *rencontre*. The bystanders closed round and prevented my carriage from proceeding. Immediately a gentleman on horseback, Mr. Onley,[1] took out of his pocket a sheet of paper from which he read a long address to his Lordship, purporting to emanate from the inhabitants of Cheltenham, recounting the great benefits which it was alleged had been conferred on the town by his Lordship having made it his residence in the winter and headquarters of his hunting establishment. The crowd then separated, and the peer gave me a nod in passing, as much as to say, this is a droll position for you, the Conservative, not able to help yourself, but accidentally made a prominent figure in a troop of my Whig satellites. All this has no doubt a reference to the representation of Cheltenham, wrested from his Lordship's grasp at the last election when Craven Berkeley was thrown out by the Conservatives; but a petition against the result is now presented on the score of bribery and corruption. It is possible the Blue member may be unseated, then the Yellows will make a vigorous effort to recover the lost seat, which, since the Reform Act passed has been treated very much as a family borough appendant to Berkeley Castle.

26th April 1848

I was told by R.W. Ford that Bishop Monk had summoned his rural deans together to consult them on a plan he had formed. I was very impressed by the extent of the Bishop's generosity. His plan is to devote a large sum, over which he has entire control, and which he might without blame appropriate to his private purposes, above £9,000, to the erection of parsonages in small benefices in the diocese.

---

1 Probably Samuel Onley, developer of Bayshill, who claimed to have dug enough brick earth to make a million bricks.

The money derived partly from the Bishop's private savings, and partly from the sale of his interest as Bishop in the manor of Horfield, near Bristol, to the Ecclesiastical Commissioners. This was a very valuable property, said to be then worth, £200,000, all of which he intended to give to the Church Commissioners, for the advantage of the Church generally, except a comparatively small sum to go towards his parsonage house fund.[1]

August 5th, 1848

Edward was engaged to go to Tysoe in Warwickshire for the christening of the first born child of William Howell who is now curate there. His marriage is the result of long attachment; but the lady brought him little fortune, and his father makes no pecuniary provision for him. It is true that William displeased his father by his violence and eagerness of temper at the time of his sister Emmeline's strange misconduct, or derangement, whichever it might be; but the young man's general deportment is free from reproach. Howell, I grieve to say, has failed generally in the paternal duties leaving his eldest son and daughter without due provision, and not making himself beloved by his younger daughters.[2]

August 24th, 1848

Rose and breakfasted early: left home in our chariot with post horses to attend the consecration of the church at Cerney Wick. When we arrived within a mile of Cirencester we crossed the turnpike road leading from that town to Barnsley and Bibury and then passed on our right the residence of Mr. Bowly a gentleman who married as his second wife, my cousin Maria Whalley. He is a farmer, brewer, and man of business taking a lead in the management of the Cirencester Union, and in all questions relating to agriculture and the general prosperity of the country. He has very right and moderate views, and being able to express himself

---

1 Bishop Monk's Horfield Trust is still thriving today and the trustees meet twice a year to settle business in Bristol, spending the money the kind Bishop allocated for their hotel expenses by giving a small luncheon party.

2 A sad entry of this date shows that Howell subsequently had some troubles with his family. Witts was nearly always kind and understanding with young people, in whose welfare he was interested.

in public with much facility, clearness, and sound reasoning, he has acquired deservedly a considerable reputation as a leading man in this district.

When we reached the Thames and Severn Canal we deviated from the turnpike road to the right and soon arrived at the little hamlet of Cerney Wick. It was a few minutes after 11 o'clock when we arrived, the service having begun on the punctual Bishop presenting himself before he was expected. Waller and I put on our surplices, hoods and scarves in a cottage by the road side and after some little difficulty obtained seats for ourselves and the ladies near the pulpit. The first lesson was read by Mr. Howman, the Rector of Barnsley and Rural Dean of Fairford Deanery, who is also honorary Canon of Bristol. The second lesson was read by Mr. Powell the incumbent of Cirencester and the sermon was preached by the vicar Canon Ford. It was the same sermon he preached when Stow church was re-opened for divine service after its recent restoration. The churchyard was consecrated, the cricket tent from Stow being set up to shelter the Bishop from the passing showers. Nothing can be more suitable, unpretending and simple than this little church. The architect, Mr. St. Aubyn of a good Cornish family, and nephew of Mrs. Marmaduke Vavasour was present and well deserved the compliments he received. Many years ago he was a pupil of our County Surveyor Mr. T. Fulljames of Gloucester, and was clerk of the works during the building of Edwards College, South Cerney, erected as a refuge for the wives and daughters of poor Gloucestershire clergymen deceased.

Among the clergy present was my son, (who had slept at Cirencester after visiting the Agricultural College and dined with the Bowlys,) and Matthew Hale Estcourt, now curate to his father near Tetbury, where a second and newly erected church[1] was consecrated by the Bishop yesterday.

All adjourned to a tent, borrowed from the Cirencester Archery Club where were congregated a large party seated at two long tables with a cross or high table. Canon Ford commended his excellent curate Mr. Mangin, who seems very popular with the parishioners.[2]

---

1 St. Saviour's, Tetbury, by S.W. Daukes, now redundant and in the care of the Redundant Churches Fund as an unspoiled example of Tractarian arrangement.

2 An example of pluralism: Canon Ford resided in his vicarage at Little Rissington.

September 20th, 1848

With Canon Ford looked at recent alterations in the church at Stow, which are carried, we thought, rather too far. The Rector (Hippisley) with the advice and assistance of his friend Mr. Wiggin (vicar of Hampnett), whose taste leads him much in the line of medieval architecture and church decoration, has been enriching the chancel by painting the sedile a rich blue colour on which in gold are painted the sacred monogram, perpetually repeated with stars, etc. Above the Communion table, on the wall, on each side of the East window are inscribed in ancient Gothic letters the ten commandments. All this is Wiggin's own handiwork. The picture of the Crucifixion, presented some years ago no longer blocks up the East Window and is removed to the body of the church. [1]

April 14th, 1850 [2]

A virtuous loving wife, tender mother, good daughter, kind-mistress friendly neighbour, unaffectedly pious, patient and charitable, excellent in the management of her family, attentive to poor neighbours, prudent, amiable and sensible. [3]

September 19th, 1850

The Bishop, being informed that several candidates for confirmation were prepared to take the Holy Sacrament[4] kindly promised to confirm them at the close of morning prayer. There was a very great gathering on this occasion which was to Ford's heart's content and the realization of a day dream long indulged. Mr. Francis Niblett the architect by whom the plan for enlargement of the church was furnished, was present. Henry Ford (Canon Ford's son) occupied the desk. In the newly built aisle was seated Mr. J. Bennet, at whose cost the aisle had been erected. There has only been increased room to the extent of twenty five sittings, but the

---

1 Mr. Wiggin is well-known for painting the chancel of his church at Hampnett, a complete scheme which still survives.

2 Francis Witts's wife Margaret died this day.

3 There is no doubt they were very attached to each other; she possessed the qualities he admired.

4 This was the day of the re-opening of Canon Ford's church at Little Rissington after its restoration. Ford was so excited he had planned for unconfirmed persons to receive communion much to Witts's disapproval, who consulted the Bishop's chaplain.

unsightly pews have been removed and very commodious open stalls substituted, the ends being worked with napkin pattern. There is a new carved stone pulpit. The triple Early English lancet window in the chancel is a very interesting remain, and if the windows (lancet) on the north side were restored to correspond with those on the south, the chancel would be a chaste and elegant specimen of its style, separated from the nave by a pointed Early English arch. The communion table is considerably raised and the ladies of Ford's family have enriched it with beautiful embroidery.

From the church the Bishop and clergy betook themselves to the pretty gardens of the Rectory. Good Mr. Bennet and his amiable wife had prepared a copious repast for all the young people ... in the spacious stable yard behind Mr. Bennet's farmhouse.

September 20th, 1850

I have been superintending the fixing of a coped, incised stone over the vault where my wife is buried outside the north[1] end of Upper Slaughter church. The work has been well executed in the durable Forest of Dean stone by Edwards, a skilful mason of Didbrook, who having worked at Toddington under the direction of Lord Sudeley has learnt to use the sculptor's chisel well. The coped stone, weighing nearly a ton, with an antique cross in bold relief, is copied accurately from the Revd. Paget's little pamphlet on monumental memorials.

October 7th, 1850

Had a good view of Gambier Parry's new church[2] erected on a commanding bank near his mansion. It's tapering spire is approaching to completion. The building will be a prominent object to the country round. The benefit to the immediate neighbourhood from this excellent person's excellent deed cannot fail to be great.

---

1 Witts says north; perhaps the stone now at the east has been moved, when the mortuary chapel was built by Francis Niblett to contain his own tomb.
2 Witts, on his way to Lydney, observes the progress of Highnam church.

October 10th, 1850

A long walk with Bathurst through beautiful Forest scenery which command extensive views of the Severn and the country on the opposite bank, Berkeley Hill, Oldbury etc. with the background of hills, Stinchcombe, Uley Bury, Nibley. We followed the road through a wide coppice which brought us to a sylvan waste, known as The Tufts, every step in which presented a lovely forest scene, the irregular ground, the rude cart-tracks, the furze and fern, the magnificent yew trees, the well-grouped beeches, the fine healthy oaks, offered at each step for a study for the landscape painter ... here and there a browsing donkey, or two or three scared sheep, and a fine tall and aged forester, or a fearless girl mounted on a donkey crossed our path. We had to pick our way through bog and thicket but little difficulties surmounted enhanced the pleasure. Passed some recent steam machinery with buildings in a lovely nook in the dense wood, where a shaft is being sunk for a coal mine. The noise of the wheels, with the busy movements of the swarthy workmen, and the appearance of a tall chimney, were all appropriate to the valley through which glided a stream seeking the Severn. Now it is traversed by a tram road, being the line of the Severn and Wye railway. It's highest point is central in the Forest of Dean, and thence it conveys coal and iron ore to Lydney on the Severn on the one hand, and to Lydbrook on the Wye on the other. This company pays a heavy sum as rent per tonnage to Bathurst for passing over his property.

October 11th, 1850

Before leaving I inspected some curiosities discovered a few years since in the mansion house, where some alterations were in progress. In a small cavity in a wall, behind a wainscot, were found a sacramental chalice and paten, with a number of Roman Catholic devotional books and a set of single sermons, chiefly of the date 1685 to 1688 preached at the chapels of James II and his Queen. The presumption is that all were secreted after the Revolution of 1688 by some chaplain of the Papist proprietor Sir John Wynter.

March 31st, 1851.

Mr. Dent, the High Sheriff, with Mr. Harvey of Winchcombe as his chaplain, performed his duties satisfactorily, and personally to me with great politeness. The cortege of Saturday last had been a very ostentatious and expensive affair. A breakfast at Sudeley

Castle, at which were present the personal intimates of the High Sheriff, with a large gathering of Yeomanry, farmers, tradesmen, etc. on horseback and in carriages. The guests attended their host in a long retinue to Cheltenham, where at midday a sumptuous collation awaited them in the Town Hall, Regent Street. A long procession left Cheltenham for Gloucester where they arrived at three. There then appear to have been dinners at the Bell Hotel and the Kings Head. All this is a bad precedent as regards future holders of the office. Much was the excess of those regaled at the High Sheriff's expense, and many the midnight stragglers wending their way homeward after copious libations.

April 29th, 1851

Rose at 5 a.m. after taking a cup of coffee and a slight breakfast left home in my phaeton at 6.15, arriving at the Great Western Station at Cheltenham at 8 a.m. where I was joined by my son who had ridden from Stanway. We reached Gloucester before 9 and repaired to the Bell Hotel. Much difficulty in procuring a conveyance to Highnam, all the carriages and horses having been engaged for some days. My good brother magistrate Mr. Wintle readily agreed to take us in his fly. Though somewhat feeble through age he retains all his amiability of character and good sense. We drove to the mansion of Gambier Parry whither carriages were resorting from all quarters. It was half past 10 o'clock and the laity and ladies took their seats in the church. The clergy remained to receive the Bishop. Parry's spacious mansion stands on a gentle eminence overlooking the vale of Gloucester. The taste of the owner is embellishing his property by improvement of the grounds, planting, gardening, and the erection of cottages, farmhouses, lodges etc. In a large billiard room I noticed a choice collection of modern watercolour paintings. The vestibule was crowded with clergy of whom nearly a hundred attended and of these eighty were attired in surplices, the rest of which number were myself and my son, in the gowns of academical degrees. I should have had no objections to the surplice, but it was left an open question, the Bishop preferring the gown and wisely for the surplice is viewed as a symbol of ultra High Church or Puseyism, and in these days of dissention what offends the weak brethren had better be avoided. The preponderance of High Church clergy was great on this occasion which could be called Tractarian. The Bishop arrived looking ill and complaining of having been seriously indisposed with chest complaints. To a person in rude health the fatigue of three consecrations in three days would be very tiring: yesterday the newly re-erected church of St. Michael in the city of Gloucester creditably executed after the designs of Fulljames and Waller: to-morrow a small simple church at Hucclecote: to-day Highnam. The Bishop went in his carriage to the church and the clergy walked in pairs a distance of several hundred yards by a gravel walk, the surpliced clergy preceding those in gowns.

This beautiful church is the tribute of a fond affection to the memory of a beloved wife and the dedication to the Holy Innocents has a reference to children who were snatched from loving parents in earliest infancy or who did not come to the birth. Mrs. Parry's bust fills a niche in the wall of a little chapel. Nothing can be more beautiful and rich than the interior of the church.

At the Bell at Gloucester I refreshed myself with a sandwich and a glass of negus and left the railway station starting at 4.40 p.m. I found my servants and carriage waiting for me at the Plough at Cheltenham. My servants had come at their own cost by railway to Gloucester that Charles might see the city, which he had never before visited and both walked to Highnam to witness as much of the proceedings there as might be permitted. I reached home at 8 p.m.[1]

March 16th, 1852

Breakfasted at the Bell Hotel with Purnell and Mullings, M.P.[2] Mullings has been solicited to take office under Lord Derby, and to fill the important post of Chief Secretary to the Poor Law Commission; but peremptorily declined on various grounds — an apprehension that his health might suffer from the labours of a heavy working place — a strong feeling on the protection of agricultural produce, in which he might probably come to a different judgement from the Premier.

Thence to the Shire Hall, County business but nothing of peculiar interest. I conducted as usual the financial department; on some small points Mr. D. Ricardo exhibited his usual disposition to oppose even the smallest and most reasonable claims on the county rates.

1 Quite a good day for a man approaching seventy.
2 Joseph Randolph Mullings M.P. for Cirencester from 1848-1859: formerly Joseph Pitt's solicitor.

Before dinner, with the two Purnells, Lysons and my son, visited the Docks and shipping, also the great work now in hand for widening the canal near Llanthony, being much interested in the labours now in progress as to excavation, noticing the boldness and the ingenuity of the workmen, their steadiness and energy, and the judicious application of the machinery and tools employed. Ancient sewers belonging to Llanthony Abbey, old stone coffins, and pillars and fragments of masonry are frequently laid bare.

March 18th, 1852

I arrived at the Police Station in Cheltenham where I found the Chief Constable's (Lefroy) open carriage waiting to convey me to his house at Swindon. Drove thither by the back road passing Maule's Elm, all very much altered in the lapse of years by the increase of building in the suburbs, improved roads, and the line of the railway. The village of Swindon with its manor house, its ancient church restored, its parsonage, and two or three lesser residences the property of Mr. Surman, in one of which the Chief Constable resides, is a pretty, rural, quiet hamlet embosomed in trees. Lefroy was fortunate in selecting this house on his marriage as it is within half an hour's walk, or ten minutes drive of his Constabulary office. It is near the church. The wealthiest neighbour is Mr. Surman, one of the legatees of the miser banker of Gloucester, Jemmy Wood. He is unmarried but has changed his name from Goodlake, and has a sister living with him, a pleasing person. It is strange how women accommodate themselves to a change of circumstances better than men. Miss Goodlake looks the lady, Mr. Surman does not look the gentleman. He was clerk to his kinsman the banker, and now possesses at Swindon a good estate with a handsome and large house, for the most part newly built, situate in very enjoyable pleasure grounds, bordered at a distance by the Bristol and Birmingham Railway, and commanding beautiful views of the surrounding hills. In these grounds I walked with Lefroy, who introduced me to Mr. Surman, whom we found playing billiards with Mr. Agg in an iron billiard room in the grounds. Mr. and Mrs. Agg were staying with the Lefroys. They have let their place, Hewletts, and are going for a twelvemonth to sea bathing places. At half past six Lefroy's small dining room contained a large party including Lady Steel whose husband finds Cheltenham more pleasant as a residence than Mickleton Manor.[1] Cards and music in the evening.

1 Threatened with demolition in 1976.

March 29th, 1852

Attended the Assizes. The High Sheriff, Mr. Winchcombe Howard Hartley, of Old Sodbury, a gentleman of large fortune, appeared in a very handsome equipage and cortege, being himself unusually resplendent in a garb of late disused by his predecessors in office, being attired in a splendid court dress, blue velvet coat, with huge cut steel buttons, bay for the hair, embroidered waistcoat, black satin breeches and appendages to match.

April 12th, 1852

Mr. Moore, surgeon, called in the evening to ask for information whether any recent Act of Parliament had passed forbidding the interment of deceased persons within the walls of churches. I am not aware of any such prohibition as relates to the country at large. Restrictions are laid upon Metropolitan interments. The doubt had arisen as to the burial of Lord Dynevor who died rather suddenly at Barrington Park on Good Friday of an attack of gout at the heart.

April 12th, 1852

Broome arrived on his pony, having gone to meet the foxhounds at Guiting.

April 17th, 1852

After an early breakfast my son, with Broome, took his departure for Stanway in his open carriage, setting out so early that my beloved grandson might proceed soon after he reached his home to meet the coach at Beckford Inn to be conveyed back to Parkhall after his short holidays. I was thankful for having enjoyed so much of the dear boy's company, and that he had been allowed to remain with me to the last moment.

April 17th, 1852

A letter to Sophy from Laura Howell was written on the day before her intended marriage to the German musician, Hubert Engels, in which it is pretty plain that she repents of the rash engagement without her father's approval: yet she speaks of the affair as settled, and as likely to lead to her future happiness and sends her new address in Bonn. A letter from her father to Edward a day later, shows that the ill-omened marriage did not take place, being postponed for a week. It is altogether a lamentable affair, whatever the issue.

April 19th, 1852

Wrote to the Brothers Jessop, nurserymen of Cheltenham, allowing them to insert my name as one of the patrons of the coming exhibition of poultry at Cheltenham, also ordered a few dahlia plants for my flower garden.

Wrote to Turner, fishmonger, London, for a dish of fish for my dinner party on Thursday.

Received a letter from Mr. Clarke, architect, Gloucester, applying for my subscription to a work he is preparing — a popular account of Llanthony Abbey. He is the author of an architectural History of Gloucester, lately published, and not without merit. [1]

May 1st, 1852

Received a letter from the clerk of the Lieutenancy for this county asking whether, if I should be appointed Deputy Lieutenant, I would qualify and act in that capacity. I replied in the affirmative, and stated my qualifications in land. Country squires, well qualified and permanently resident are few in this district. I presume I am called on as a man in harness and still equal to work as a magistrate or otherwise in the transaction of public business.

[1] The *Architectural History of Gloucester* by John Clarke, 1850.

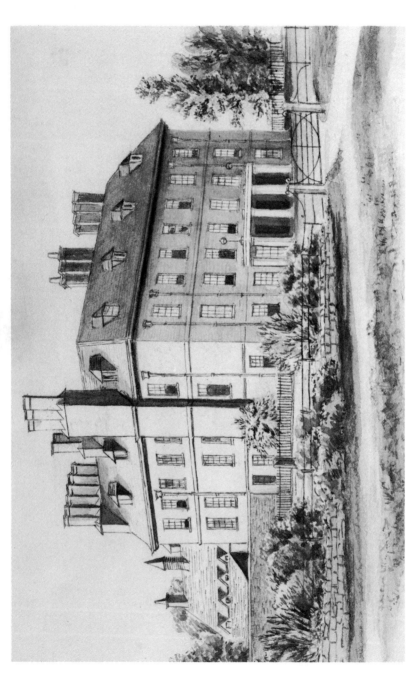

Lydney Park, the seat of Charles Bathurst

INDEX OF PEOPLE AND PLACES

Page numbers in italics refer to
illistrations or their captions.
Footnotes are indicated by the letter n
following the page number.